LILY'S OWN

Stories of a Childhood

by

Nadine Pedron

Copyright © 2013 by Nadine Pedron

Published in the United States by the Word Project Press of Sonora, CA.

Requests for permission to make copies of any part of this work should be submitted online at
info@wordprojectpress.com

Credits:

Author Photo: EGP
Cover Design: Melody W. Baker

ISBN-13: 978-0-9890682-2-2
ISBN-10: 0-9890682-2-6

Author's Note

"Lily's Own" is an autobiographical novel—a merging of autobiographical and fiction elements. While the stories are rooted in actual, real life events and the central plotline mirrors the author's life, they have been altered, enhanced, and dramatized for artistic or thematic purposes, without pretense of exact truth.

Dedication

Dedicated to the Mrs. V's and Mr. P's—teachers of the world who change the trajectory of students' lives in positive and profound ways. Thank you.

Leaving Home

"Don't you stick that hateful tongue out at me, little missy," Aunt Hettie hisses, gluey bits of spit hanging from her lip. "I'm a mind to whup yore bottom."

I hate Aunt Hettie. How come she gets to sleep on the only real mattress?

"No whining, now," Mother shushes. "You can't always have your way," she whispers in my ear while she jiggles baby Nita in her lap. Arms and legs everywhere. Scrunched in, bunched up, our backsides touching. Look at Aunt Hettie's fat ol' body, flung out, taking up the whole blamed mattress. Rest of us on blanket pallets and skinny pillows. It's bumpy and achey sitting and laying on these grey-dusty, splintery floor boards, them smelling like coal oil. Our rusty flat bed truck is driving day and night, day and night, right straight through to California. Mother and Daddy, brother and sister, aunts, uncles, and cousins—all of us jammed in, leaving home, cuz there's no money, no crops, no jobs back there in Texas.

We're traveling with two busted out, rope-tied-up cardboard boxes and a buncha clanging pots wired to the top of the truck. Daddy told me just before we left home that day, his eyes looking

3

right straight into mine and his hands curled like fists on his hips, "It might look like it with this ol' truck and all, but Lily, you remember this, we're not Okies, you hear me?"

Mother finds me a spot to sit away from mean ol' Aunt Hettie. "Now, Lil, just behave yourself. I expect you to act better, now you're five. Here, take this quilt and rest a spell. Pass the time, quiet like. Maybe day dreaming, you know, or sleeping some."

I wrap up in my favorite quilt, the one Mother and her sewing circle made. Reckon I'll scrinch up my eyes and think about home. Sure miss Granpa and Granma already. I can see them standing on the porch of our little shack-like house the day we had to leave. Granma cried out loud into her apron pulled up over her face. Granpa bowed his head, shuffling his shoes in the dirt, sticking his big hand deep in his overalls pocket to get his red bandana kerchief. I held onto his knees as long as I could before mother pulled me away with her arm around me, hugging tight.

Our house back home on the farm sits up on big flat rocks hauled from the creek. My Daddy and Granpa built it for us out of big rough boards. It's got a tin roof that drips a little rain water into the house in the winter time. Plink, plink, plink into the ol' tin bucket. It has two rooms. There's a kitchen and a sitting room together and a bedroom where we all slept. Jack and me on a mattress laid on the floor across from Mother and Daddy's bed and Nita in her rocking crib. Yellow and blue flowers are dancing around on the wallpaper in there, curling up and peeling off around the bottom. Guess I helped peel a little myself one day when Mother made me sit in the corner. The chickens live outside with the outhouse and cellar.

I'm thinking now we mighta been poor folks, even before the Great Depression and the Bowl a Dust. But we never got hungry on the farm. I'm making out in my mind Granma and Granpa in their big house with the big kitchen and the big meals.

Short, round Granma is always busy. At supper time, she gathers, chops, slices, bakes, fries, sets the table and washes up all the dishes and pots and pans. After that she sweeps the floor and stacks the wood, neat and tidy over there by the big black stove. Finally, she throws all the peelings, crusts, and vegetable leavings in a bucket, carries it in both hands, kicking open the screechy screen door with her foot. She stomps clear over to the animal barn to slop the hogs, them squealing at the gate. Every day. Yes siree, even Sunday.

5

Granpa talks. And rocks. He's lean like a green string bean and taller than the tallest cornstalk out in the field. Of an evening, he folds his long body into the rocking chair that Great Grandfather built hisself a long time ago. Sitting down at his feet, I can see hairs hanging out of his long crookedy nose. Daddy says it's the Cherokee in him, that nose. Just like the blue eyes are the German in him. He's got a bouncy Adams Apple (that's what Granpa calls that bump in his neck) and a bony, pointy chin with short scratchy whiskers on it and a smattering of yellow-brown teeth, some gone in the back.

Granpa sits in that ol' cane rocker and tells good stories, the same ones over and over. I love all of them, over and over. All of us Texans like story telling. He chaws tobacco while he drawls out his words, and he makes me wait until he squirts and spits. Pitooey! That stinky juice flies right smack dab into the tall tin can sitting next to his chair. He never misses. Granma says, "Thank the Lord."

The stories are about our family, and they always have a giggly-funny part and once in awhile there's a surprise at the end. I specially like the one about me sitting on baby brother's belly, stuffing popcorn in his mouth to keep him quiet. Granpa says little Jack choked and like-to-died in the ol' Willys jeep that Daddy gunned to the floor board all the way to the hospital over in Santa Anna, where I was born. I know about that cuz Mother showed me the piece of paper that spells out my name and tells all about my birthday in nineteen-hundred and thirty-three.

I beg him for the stories, but it's hard to wait for the best parts. Sometimes I whisper the words to myself before they come out of his mouth. Granpa is selfish about his story telling though, and he sure hates me getting ahead of him. One time he heard me muttering the good part about to come up and he got purple-red in the face, smacked his hands on the arms of that ol' rocker, and growled mean-like at me. "What a dickens, you are! You hush up, hear? No more talking from you! When you get growed up, little missy smarty pants...then you can tell your own gol-dang stories."

My own. I'm remembering how I have to pinch my lips together with my fingers and sit quiet like, cross-legged, down there by his big clod-hopper boots, right next to the spitting can. I try real hard to wait for that growed-up day a-coming.

Ornery

Guess I'm a dickens, all right, least ways everybody says so. Stubborn, oo-ee, they say. And mean, too. I'm so mean and ornery my Daddy has to take a switch to me. A lot. I don't like to think on it, but I do.

My Daddy comes in from the cotton fields just before sundown. Slow, shuffly feet, skinny chin resting on his grimy buttoned-to-the-top work shirt. He's plum stove in. "Lily," his tired voice yells out. "Liiillly, I am calling you." I hear him, all right. I know I'm gonna get it. Brother Jack musta told on me for snitching the last of the chocolate cake and lying to Mother about it.

Daddy cuts the green, bendy switch from the mesquite tree in the front yard. He uses his red jackknife, and I'm watching from the porch, my knees all wibbly-wobbly. I want to holler NO! But I just wait. I wish I could wiggle under the house cuz he can't reach me there.

Sharp, hot, stinging mesquite branch in my Daddy's hand—swatting across my bare, bony legs. My breath gets all snatched up. Way down deep inside me, clear to my toes, I'm hot- burning and hating, hurting real bad and hating more. I'll show you, Daddy. I won't cry. I won't.

9

But I do finally cry. Cuz my Daddy does—at the end of the switching when he slumps down on his knees and hangs his heavy head, like praying.

In the night time, I can hear Mother and Daddy talking about me when they think I'm asleep. I keep real still under the quilt.

"Lester, what are we going to do about Lily? That little girl is so contrary. I can't imagine her saying anything except 'No', never mind what I tell her. First thing, she's got to ask why, but she's bound to argue with whatever I say. Then, Lawdy, she's going to find a way to do what she wants to anyway. She's vexin' me to death."

"I know it," Daddy says. "No use in whuppin' her any more. Just makes her meaner and meaner. Durned if I can figure out that girl. Where did she come from, do you think? She doesn't favor my side of the family. What about yours, Opal? Your kin got any children feisty as Lily?"

I can hear Mother heaving a big sigh. "I swear, not a one. The good Lord knows I try to make her mind, but I'm just too wore out now to fuss with it anymore. I'm a mind to let her do what she wants as long as she doesn't hurt anybody or make us ashamed."

It's quiet now except for Daddy's snoring and sputtering. He surely is a loud sleeper.

Wish I could sleep. I'm squishing my eyelids closed, but I can't stop thinking about them saying they don't know where I come from, how I'm not like the kinfolk. None of them.

I do sleep though, after I remember the no more whuppin' part.

Being Purty and Me Not Being

"Ugly! Poor thang. Always was." Aunt Jewel's finger is tapping the photograph of Cousin Elva Sue. Closing the fat family album, she nudges me with her elbow. "Hon, you remember your Daddy's saying: Well, she can't help it if she's ugly, but least ways she could stay home!" Heh, heh, heh. That big ol' cackle jiggles my aunt's plumpy arm flesh.

I'm over at Aunt Jewel's little house today cuz the rheumatiz has got her and Mother says now I'm big enough to help out. My aunt is a real Texan, bothered not-one-speck by saying out loud just what she thinks. And something else about Texans here about is that any talking about a woman starts with how purty she is...or is not.

While we sort the dirty laundry out on the warm smooth rocks by the wash tub, I ask her if I'm purty. She leans over, real slow like, with her hand holding her back to toss a sock into the white pile. She looks at me a good long while and then says, "Well, Lily, you're not ugly anyway. Least ways, you won't have to stay home. Heh. Heh. Heh." Her belly jiggles under her apron. "But purty? You're gonna have to work on it." She motions to me to go get the scrub board.

"Doing what, Aunt Jewel?" I'm not too

keen on working much, spying the big yellow bar of lye soap in her hand.

"Well, let's see, now." She stops to wipe the sweat off her forehead with a holey sock. "First, you better wear that bonnet when you go outside because, you know, wrinkles are surely ugly. And, remember to slather that cream all over your hands after you wash the dishes. Makes purty hands. And curly hair, good thang you got a little, but mostly it's like a limp dish rag. Now, your eyes. They's just not a pure color, you know. They's kinda just smutty-dun. Not like your mother's real blue ones. Nothing to do for it though, just like your nose. Pity about your nose. Come by it honest, though. You got that long, beaky thing from your Granpa. But the truth is, little girl, if you're not naturally purty, you got to be smart."

Back at our house, Mother cooks supper and I set the table, trying to remember about forks on the left. "Mother, you think I'm purty?"

She turns five pieces of chicken in the sizzling pan. "Honey, purty is as purty does." I know what that means. Well, she can afford to say that since she's naturally purty. But I don't want to be sugary sweet all the time just to seem like purty. When we all sit down to supper Mother remembers something else more practical. "Did ya'll know that eating the chicken neck makes you purty? Who wants it?"

I don't have much trouble getting that neck. My little sister looks just like Mother, so she doesn't need any help. Daddy and Jack just snigger into their gravy.

At evening time, sitting out on the porch, keeping warm with my skirt pulled down over my knees and tucked under my toes, I start to feel real bad. I worry about purtiness a lot. I think it's cuz my Daddy really likes purty girls, and that's why my sister is his favorite. I cry into my hands, big tears come a-slipping out, dripping down through my fingers. Daddy pushes out through the creaky screen door. "Lily, what you doing out here in the dark?"

I just can't help it. I have to tell it. I can taste a salty tear when I open my mouth to mumble it out. "Oh Daddy...I wish I was purty." He picks up his whitling off the stool by the door and drops into the ol' rocking chair. He sets to work with his pocket knife, with the light from the kitchen slanting over his shoulder. Little shavings flutter down to the porch boards and rest there in a splinter bed. I'm waiting and scrubbing off the tears.

Finally, Daddy says, "Well, Sugar Sack..." He's a thinking, and I'm feeling some better already cuz Sugar Sack is what he calls me when he feels sad and sorry about my troubles. "Here's what you do, Lil. Wish in one hand and spit in the other and see which one gets full the fastest."

My Daddy is full of sayings like that. I asked him one time where he learned them and he said they were "ol' Eddards sayings" but he didn't know who ol' Eddards was, cuz his own Daddy passed them on to him, not ol' Eddards hisself."

Anyhow, those ol' Eddards sayings stay stuck with me a good long time, specially the wishing and spitting one. But my Mother's saying was all wrong. Cuz, I'm telling you, no amount of chicken necks makes you purty.

About Religion

"Ol' time religion, ol' time religion, ol' time religion...is good enough for me!" Cousin Wanda is banging sweet chords on the ol' pianer so hard her bottom bounces up and down on the shiny swivel stool. Preacher Dale holds his Bible open on one hand and leads us with the other. Our sangin' voices are so loud, it makes my bones buzz a little.

Mother says, "We're Baptist, Hard Shell." I try to think about a hard shell. Like on the old terrapin that crawls around in the mud by the water well? Like a boiled egg...specially when its shell is hard to peel off? But Mother says, "No, not like that exactly. We're strict. Live straight by the bible, follow all the rules. You know... no gambling, no dancing, no painted faces, no drinking—so on and so forth."

Baptists round us do their baptizing in Granpa's tank, way down by the watermelon patch. It's time I was baptized, Preacher Dale tells Mother and Daddy one Sunday out on the church steps. "No, Daddy, no." I'm bawling and hanging onto his legs. "I don't want to. I'm ascared."

Daddy, squatting down to me, says not to act like a baby and straighten up, right now. He whispers in my ear. "You don't see anyone else acting scared about baptizing. Sometimes, Lily, I wonder where you come from!"

But I keep thinking about the baptizing day. Mother will tell me to put on my starchy Sunday go-to-meetin' dress and we'll all walk over to the tank with the other church folks. Granpa's tank is dark and deep in the middle and has mud that sucks your feet under. I'll hafta wade way out there to where the Preacher is waiting for me. I'll hafta hold the skirt of my purty dress so it doesn't float on top of the water. When I get to him, he'll reach round and hold the back of my neck, then pinch my nose shut and lean me way down backwards 'til my whole head is under in the black suffocating water.

My pillow is soaked with my crying every night, worrying about it. What if Preacher Dale forgets about me under there while he's praying to the Lord up in the sky? I might die.

It's gonna be tomorrow. Mother says to go to bed now, so I'll be ready early in the morning. Under the sheet, my hands prayer-pressing together, I whisper. "Now I lay me down to sleep, I pray the Lord my soul to keep. If I should die...tomorrow, I pray the Lord my soul to take." I'm ashamed to pray for what I want next, but I do, anyway. "And dear Lord, please, please save me. I can't do the baptizing.

18

Please don't make me. I'll be good, really, really good for the rest of my whole life if you don't make me. I'll get baptized one day, I promise, when I'm big and can hold my breath long enough. Puhleeze, God. Amen."

And, do you know, the good Lord does take pity on me. Preacher Dale has a spell of hard coughing and spends the day in his bed. Praise the Lord.

Not everybody is a Baptist though. Daddy tells about the Holy Rollers. "Right entertaining," he says. Every summer Mother and Daddy and the grown up kinfolks (except kids can't go, might get scared, Mother says) pack up a picnic and head out to the big tent where the Holy Rollers have their meeting.

"Almost good as a circus," and Daddy tells it so's I can almost see it. "Tent's full a people on rickety ol' chairs or sitting on the ground in the hard dirt. There's a sangin', like us, and a preacher, like us, and regular praying, too. But after a spell that preacher yells and hollers and gets those people so het up that they start ascreaming and tearing at their clothes and rolling round in the dust. Crazy people, seems to me. Why, one time, they even brought snakes!" When Daddy tells this part, he slaps his legs and bugs out his eyes. We squeal...we do, all us kids. Daddy grins and his eyes dance around. "Lordy, what a sight, those Holy Rollers. Just can't wait 'til next year, no siree."

One more thing about religion. If it's not yours, you don't belong. I learn about this in California. After those long three days and three nights on the road, our Texas flat-bed truck finally stops. We hafta live in a house all cramped up with relatives who came here before us. Mother says it's one of those fruit pickers houses, all of them lined up by the orange trees. On Saturday nights, all the Texans from round about meet at this house. We have a pot of pinto beans and corn bread and greens with hot oil and vinegar poured over them. Most of us sit on the rough wood floor, our backs propped up against the wall, eating off little white paper plates. We have a sangin' even without a pianer. When it's late and the kids are sagging on the floor, all the folks pass the hat. That means that everybody who can puts money in the hat. The family that needs it the most gets the money. It's us this time.

Pretty soon, though, Daddy only has a little jingling money left in his pockets. He's worried and ashamed that he might need the hat money again. There might not even be enough gas in the truck to get me to that school I'm s'posed to be in. The before-us relatives tell Mother that I need to be in a school. Mother says, "Well, that's a big surprise to me because Lily's not quite six yet and nobody in Texas starts school 'til seven. I'll be!"

But, we're Californians now, so Mother and Daddy find a school, not too far away, and Daddy takes me there Monday morning on his way to talk to a man about a job. "We need a job real bad," he says. Daddy, quick though, has to leave and I'm having to wait a spell on one of the chairs lined up in front of a wood table in the school office. A shiny cross is hanging on the wall behind it and a stack of papers gets held down with a blue inkwell, like the one I remember on Granma's sitting room table.

Sure is quiet, just me breathing and a big, round clock, tick-tocking in its spot over a little window. My chair's so high up I can swing my feet to that tick-tock tune. Best stop, though. Mother says school's got rules.

Pretty soon, a lady in a robe with a black hood-like bonnet comes through the door and stands right smack in front of me. She asks me if I'm Cath-o-lick. Huh. "I dunno. What's Cath-o-lick?" I ask. Robe lady's eyes get slitty. She's twisting the handkerchief she took out of her pocket round and round with her fingers while she's thinking.

"Well, then. What church do you go to?" she says, resting her hand on her hip.

Oh, okay. I know this answer. I sit up real tall and look her straight in the eye, just like Daddy says to do when growed up folks ask you a question. "We're Baptists with hard shells, ma'am."

The slitty eyes go round. She flips the hem of her robe and marches into the next room to whisper to another robe lady. Then, she leans around the door and crooks up her pointer finger at me so I'll follow her down a long white hall. I can hear her shoes tap-tapping on the concrete floor, her feet kicking up her robe front and back. She leads me down the middle of the biggest place I ever saw—no feet noises on the long rug we walk on. Feels so still. It's like the storm cellar back home. Smells like the candles we light down there too. I hafta lean my head way back to see the top of the tall, tall ceilings and windows that let in a little light through some green and blue colored glass. There's a bigger-than-me wood cross up there and a lot of what Mother calls pee-yous, all lined up in shiny wood. It's gotta be a church. Lord A Mighty! There's Jesus hisself! He's standing right still, hanging his head, with blood dripping down from his hands and feet. Is he real?

Ol' robe lady has to grab my arm and pull me outta there through a door that's right next to dead Jesus. She looks down at me with her finger and her stiff black hood-bonnet pointing out every word. "Young lady, this school is for Catholics only. Please tell that to your parents." The skinny pointer finger shows me where I should sit on the top of some crumbly rock steps in back of the church. "You may wait right here for your father." I feel a little breeze from her robe when she turns around, right smart like, and marches away.

It's the gol-danged-est long wait I ever had in my life. Enough time to feel the blues. That's Mother's word she says means sorta sad. Lordy, my bottom is tired and my eyes are drying out from trying not to blink, so I don't miss the first sight of Daddy coming down the driveway in the ol' flat-bed truck. I can hear Mother telling me, "Just shake the blues when they come on you."

Sure is cold enough out here to shake. It's even starting to get dark.

Can't wait to tell him. I'm gonna run down these steps and jump in the front seat and tell him, with my eyes dancing around. "Daddy, guess what? Cath-o-licks in California are almost as entertaining as the Holy Rollers in Texas!"

Our Own House

I do finally go to school, after all's said and done. But it takes awhile. Mother says I missed a whole year if you go by California school rules. See, we have to get in that ol' truck one more time and leave Fresno cuz Daddy's job in the fruit fields plum plays out and there is just enough money in his pocket to buy gas so we can head on out to find a new job. Uncle Arthur says maybe there's work to the north. By the time we get to this little town called Pleasanton and find us a place to live, Mother figures it's too late for school.

We're right happy in our new house, cuz we don't hafta stay with the relatives any more. Daddy says it feels like God smiled on us and brought about a little miracle.

It happens like this. Soon as our tired family pulls up in town after all those miles from Fresno, we spy the pretty white church on the corner of First Street. Daddy stops the truck around the back, spits on both hands and slicks back his hair. After he smoothes down his shirt and kicks the dirt off his boots on the running board, he walks with his straw hat in his hand to the front door of a house where Daddy figures the Preacher lives.

"Howdy," Daddy says, when the door opens up. Well, when Daddy comes outta that door he's smiling and walking tall. Turns out the Preacher knows about a job, and it's right across the street and blamed if a little house don't go with it.

"Hallelujah, Lester," Mother fairly sings it out when he gets the job and we get our house.

Mrs. Parks is the rich ol' lady who gives us a job and a place to live. She says every one of us will have a job. Daddy will take care of the big yard and the animals in the back pasture and fix up broken stuff in the big, big house where she lives. One more thing. He'll drive her places and keep her car up to snuff. Mother will clean the big, big house and wash her clothes and make the meals for Mrs. Parks. And me and Jack and Nita will do odd jobs. I don't know what odd jobs means yet.

Our new house is made of out of wood boards like our house in Texas, and the roof leaks rain the same. Mother and Daddy sleep in a bed in their own bedroom and Nita and me sleep together on a mattress in a big closet like place. Jack gets the screened-in side porch with a cot and lots of quilts. There's a bathroom inside that flushes, and the kitchen has a wood stove and a real big ice box. And gollee, there's a sitting room with shiny linoleum on a floor that slants down just right for rolling marbles.

Turns out one odd job for me is to watch Mr. Parks over in the big, big house when Daddy takes Mrs. Parks out in the car. Seems like he's older than Grandpa, sitting slumped over in a wheel chair, his grey haired head resting on his chest.

Mrs. Parks tells me, "Lily, just sit here on the couch next to him and watch him breathe. See...chest and belly... in and out."

"Yes Ma'am. Then what?"

"That's all. I won't be very long. If you get worried about anything, just run over to your house and get your Mother."

In and out, in and out. Better not blink, I might miss one of those ins or outs. Lordy, after a while my neck is hurting and my eyes are itching. Okay, I'll sneak a rub, just a little rub. Now, again, in and out, in and out, and, and ...and...

"Mother, Mother! I'm screaming and slamming through the door to our kitchen. " No in, no in, no in!"

No house, no house, I just know it. We'll lose our house. No jobs, no jobs, no place to live. Cuz I didn' do my odd job right.

Mother and Daddy bring Mrs.Parks home from the funeral in the pretty white church across the street. No jobs, no jobs. In and out, in and out. I'm worrying to death.

Mrs. Parks gets out of the car, leaning on her cane. She motions me over and asks me to come in and sit with her in the big, big house. I sit on the couch where I rubbed my eyes.

"Lily. Please forgive me. I gave you a job I shouldn't have." Mrs. Parks dabs at her eyes with a little white, lacey handkerchief and reaches over from her highback chair to hold my hands in her blue veiny ones. "It was his time," she says. "You did nothing wrong. God decided it was his time. He went to meet his maker in peace, with a sweet little girl watching over him. Thank you."

Sweet. Nobody in my whole life ever, ever called me sweet.

"Uh." I'm scared to say it. "Uh, Mrs. Parks, uh, can we keep our jobs and odd jobs and our house?"

And do you know what she said, real quiet like, wiping at her eye?

"Of course, dear girl. And your next odd job right now is to smile and go outside and climb a tree or skip a rope or race, free like the wind."

Books

The big ol' glinty, sharp-pointy butcher knife is raised up in the air over his head and his other hand is way up high too, looking like he's saying "Hallelujah, Praise be to God!" This man looks like God, with his long white beard and ol-timey white robes. Mother says the words at the bottom of the picture say "Abraham and Isaac on Mount Moriah." I wonder if Isaac is the little boy tied to the pile of sticks with his eyes closed. I can't read those words, but I stare at the picture every chance I can. It's the scariest thing I ever saw in my life. After Mother tells me the story about Abraham being tested by God and all, it is worse. What Daddy could kill his boy—no matter who told him to.

But I keep going back and back to that Bible, turning the pages, looking for more pictures and any words I can read. It isn't just any book, it's THE book. That's what Daddy calls it...maybe cuz it is the only book in our house. It's black with gold print on the cracked leather that says "Holy Bible" and my Daddy's whole name is printed at the bottom. On the back page, my mother wrote my whole name and the day I was born and Jack's name and the day he was born. But Nita's name isn't there. We have been

29

lying to her, telling her she is an orphan and ha-ha, this proves it. She screams and cries when we tell her one time that we picked her up along side the road when we drove through New Mexico. She tries to kick and bite us when we tell her that's why she's so dark-colored, and we're not. Mother shushes Jack and me with a swat on the bottom and rocks little runt Nita, telling her, "I just ran out of time to write names in the Bible by the time you got born, sweetheart."

I love books. Funny books are the first we have besides the Bible. The best thing in the world is to have a big stack of funny books, traded with other kids on Friday after school, and then all day Saturday to read them. Mickey Mouse and Bugs Bunny and Archie and Veronica and best of all——Plastic Man. When the last funny book gets plopped on the done pile, I always feel so sad…sorta lonesome-like and grumpy.

Want to know one of the most wonderful days of my life? It is hot summer when school is out. Mother tells me I am old enough to walk to the library by myself! It's six blocks after Fruden's Grocery store on Main street where I get to go when we run out of milk and bread. I feel like running from our house all the way, but I keep having to wipe the sweat off my face with the sash on my dress, so I slow down, walking big steps so I don't land on any break-your-mother's-back cracks in the sidewalk.

The Li- brr- ary ("Not li-berry," my teacher says) is brick all the way around with lots of windows and heavy doors with chunky gold handles. I have to pull real hard and stick my foot in first to hold my place, so I can slide in. It's so cool on my face, and I love that smell. It's the book smell. There are two more doors, but they're wide open and when I step in there, books are all around me. Just look! Shelves low, shelves high—all lined up with a million-trillion books! Long shiny wood tables are in the middle of the room, and the Li-brrr-ar-ian is sitting at a desk. My sandals make way too much noise on the floor cuz nothing else is moving in here. Mother said I could look at books all afternoon, and the librarian says I can even take some home. I can't believe it. It's better than Christmas.

I go to the library almost every day. I don't even need to trade funny books any more. And I never open that Bible again.

The Worst Best Day

I'm wondering if I could skip for a whole mile. That's how far Daddy says it is from school to home. I'm so happy today, I bet I could do it. It's not the kind of happy like when you find a dime shining in a gutter or even when your birthday comes and you get just what you asked for. See, today is bubbly, like the water in Mother's teakettle just before it whistles. A bunch of good things happened. It's the last day of school for the summer, and I got some A grades on my report card with a little note to my parents from Mrs.Garabaldi telling them I am a good student. They will be so surprised.

Mother will be at home (the very best thing of the day), cooking ham hocks and lima beans in the cast iron pot. The new tire swing is waiting, real still on its rope that Daddy tied to the Sycamore tree. And, guess what, the Lone Ranger is coming on the radio tonight, 7:00 o'clock. Yes sirree! Just the best day.

I jump up the three bouncy steps when I get home to make up for cheating a little on the skipping part back there aways. I land on our splintery porch. This house is a brown boxy one with wood shingles on the sides, way out on Rose Avenue right next to the race track. It's our

33

second house in purty...uh...pretty little Pleasanton town where, thank the Lord, Daddy finally got a job with the Jackson and Perkins rose nursery. Mother says we're real lucky to be renting from Mr. Carlsen because he's got so much money that he might not mind if we have to be late or a little skimpy on the payment sometimes.

"Hey Jack! Hey Nita! Where are you?" I holler out, running around to the backyard to find them. There's Jack dragging a big old stick along the dirt, stomping chunky clods with his bare feet. Skinny-kneed Nita follows right along behind him. She's twisting the hem of her yellow daisy flour sack dress with her left-hand fingers, sort of in time with the right hand thumb-sucks in her mouth .

"Hey ya'll, wanna play?"

Jack squints up into the sun, shading his eyes with his dusty hand. "Play what?"

"I dunno yet."

Jack starts to pick up his stick again.

"Guess what! There's a tar truck on the street down by the Palmer's house. Let's ask Mother if we can go on down there."

"I doh wanna," Nita mumbles around her thumb, looking through loose little curls hanging over her eyebrows. Rats. She's gonna be bratty.

"Oh, come on. I'll pull you in the wagon, okay?"

"Uh, uh, you pull too fast."

"I promise." One hand is on my heart and the other is grabbing hers—quick, careful not to touch the slimy thumb-sucking one.

The truck is smoking and getting hotter the closer we get to it. The thing is crusty black all over, and I think about the Tar Baby story. The tar truck workers are down the road a piece, having a drink of water from the neighbor's hose. See, I knew this was the best day. Cuz now we can look for the little plops of tar that fell on the road when they were working here. Jack finds the first one, and then I find a bunch too. "Be careful. It might still be too hot," I yell to Jack, too late to stop him from sticking his tongue on a piece of gluey, gummy, shiny tar. "It's good," he says, and pushes the glob into his cheek. I test mine with my finger before I put it into my mouth. I nudge Jack with my elbow and use my deep voice. "Chawin', huh, Jack?" We swagger down the road and chaw on awhile, spitting out on the road just like Granpa, setting off little sizzles on the summer street.

Rambling on back home, our black tongues making us dream about some cherry Koolaid, I try to think up a new "play-like." The girls at school say "pretend" and I'm trying to get used to that word like a lot of other words that folks say funny in California. But Jack and Nita wouldn't even know what I was talking about. "Hey, I know. Let's play-like we're going on a trip...maybe back to Texas for a visit." Jack sorta likes this idea, his tow head a bobbing.

Nita takes out her thumb to whine, "I doh wanna."

Oh Lordy, what a durn baby! I can hear Mother talking in my head though. "Now, Lily, she is the baby in the family. Have a little pity, hear me?"

"Yes you do, Nita," I say sweet-like. "Don't you wanna see your cousins?"

"No. We can't really see 'em." She plugs her thumb back in.

"I know, but play-like is fun anyway. So, okay, first we need to pack up our suitcases. Let's get that old one out of the shed." We play-like pack and play-like set off driving all day and all night, sitting in the rusty little wagon out in the front yard. We visit cousins and see the country and eat hamburgers and swig Nehies in cafes along the way and finally come on back home to California.

"I wanna go in the house," Nita blubbers. She's through with play-like. We gather up the old cardboard suitcase and head on in.   Nita drags her feet, whimpering "I'm tiii...erd." I'm biting my tongue.

"Hey Nita, we could carry you in...in the suitcase." She stomps her foot "no" and I can see a tantrum coming on. I feel myself turning off Mother's voice.

"Jack, let's put her in!" Jack and I try to push her over to the suitcase lying down flat in the dirt, but she's screaming now and it's not going to be easy. "We can pick her up, Jack. Open it up and get ready." Little arms and legs, seems like everywhere, are kicking and clutching at us. We pry her off us, shove her in, stuff in the parts hanging out and close the lid as far as it will go. We huff and puff and pick it up and struggle on a few feet with her bawling to beat the band. Jack and me, we start laughing and joking about the little pip squeak squirming. It tickles us watching Nita punch around in there.

Craaack! The old case splits open at the bottom and Nita comes busting out. We're still laughing so hard that we don't see it right away.

Nita's down there on the ground, her head on a big old grey rock. Blood is running down her curls and her nose and her daisy dress. She's not moving, not one single part of her.

"Mother, Mother!" I scream and scream. My throat is burning. I'm running, stumbling, falling down before I can get to the house.

Mother comes flying down the steps to meet me, apron strings flapping in the air.

She races to Nita. So fast, but oh-so gently, she cradles her bleeding little head into the bend of one elbow, gathers her arms and legs into the other and lurches from side to side until she can finally stand up.

"You're in charge," Mother yells to me as she staggers to the car with Nita dangling in her arms.

They're gone now. To the hospital. I tell Jack to get down and kneel in the dirt with me. "We gotta pray hard 'til they get back. Pray. Pray Jack, that Nita's not dead." At the sound of the dead word, we both start crying.

"Are we sinners, Lil?" Tears are making little white streaks down his smudgy, scrinched up face. "Did we kill Nita?"

"Don't worry, Jack. God knows it's not your fault. It's me. I'm the oldest. I'm supposed to take care of you and Nita." Doesn't Mother's voice in my head always tell me so? What's wrong with me?

We whisper out there in the yard to God, over and over, 'til it's near dark. Jack wants to get up, but I don't let him. I just tell him to sit back down and keep a-praying.

I hear it. A crunchy sound on the gravel. Headlights. The car door slams. Mother calling. I squeeze my eyes to keep them shut. I can't stop shaking and rocking. Jack runs.

Oh, Lord, I have to go in there. The screen door scrapes when I open it into the bright, hot kitchen where the ham hocks and beans are cold on the table. Where the radio sits...the Lone Ranger long gone. Where Mother leans back heavy against the counter, Jack's head pressing against her waist. Where Nita sits on a chair, a big white gauze-thing wrapped around her curly head and a cone clutched in her hand, strawberry ice cream dripping down her grimy little sucking thumb.

What's for Lunch?

First I get the baloney, round and pink, careful to find the slices not too crinkly round the edges. Then white gummy bread, and salad dressing, if there's any left in the jar. I layer it all up and make the edges match. Then I fold it up in a piece of Langendorf bread wrapper and get a big paper grocery bag from the drawer. I need to rustle around in the catch-all drawer to find the scissors to cut it with. After I whack off the top part, almost clear down to the bottom I lay the sandwich in. Oops, forgot the carrot. Throw it in next to the sandwich. Fold the bag over and under until it's almost the size of a little, store-bought, pinked top, real lunch bag—like the ones Nancy and Judy bring to school. Their mothers write their names on the bag with little curlicues and hearts, and after lunch they throw away the bag in the lunch room garbage can. Mine needs to last a week, so I'll have to hide it in my jacket to take home since it's only Monday. One time I ask Mother if I can have real lunch bags, but I am sorry I do, cuz then Mother's eyes look sad when she says no, that we have to be real careful with our money.

Miss Barber is our third grade teacher. She wears high-heel shoes every day and has her hair rolled up in the front. Her lipstick is pink and her fingernails are "Stoplight Red." Once when she told me to get a pencil out of her bottom drawer, I saw the name on the bottle and the price sticker said 35 cents! I could buy a whole bunch of lunch bags for that, I think.

Miss Barber stands stiff as a board and has lots of rules for third graders. If you break one she gives you a Dutch Rub on the top of your head, being real careful to tuck her painted nails under her bony knuckles before she attacks, scrubbing fast back and forth until your scalp burns. I never get one of those Dutch Rubs, but on the day I get sick and throw up on her shiny shoes I think for sure I will get singed by those hot, hard knuckle bones. I think she forgets though, cuz she is so busy scrubbing her shoe with a balled up wet paper towel that I have to run and get for her.

Today we're doing Round Robin reading. That's when you all take turns, and you know exactly when you're going to be next to read. I'm sweating because there's a word I don't know. Well, I do know it, but I don't know how to say it exactly. One time, everybody laughed when I read "island" like it looks. I don't want to take any chances this time. The word in the paragraph I'm going to read is "nearer." So, is it near...*er*, or *nee*...ar? This is important to me. Lucky for me, my paragraph is last, so I'm practicing, whispering to myself using both ways to say it, but I still can't tell.   I'm desperate by the time Henry Gruber sounds out the last word of his part. But...hallelujah, thank you Lord, I'm saved by the bell. The lunch bell.

We grab our lunches and race down the steps to the cafeteria. Pulling open that big thick metal door to the lunch room takes three of us, and boy, do we let go quick and run fast to get in. Last year, Sonny Silva didn't quite make it before the monster thing whammed shut. A few months later, we had a big assembly where Mr. Benton called up Sonny to the stage and handed him a jar with his pointer finger in it, floating around in pickling juice. We all clapped, glad it wasn't us.

Judy and Patty and I slide down the bench to sit together. I unfold my big ugly bag, trying not to let it show too much. I reach down in there for my sandwich and come up with a ...Milky Way bar? I can't believe it. This can't be mine. Being careful with our money means no candy bars. Maybe our lunch bags got mixed up. My mouth is watering for that candy and my fingers play with the crackly wrapper awhile before I get up. I find Miss Barber standing by the wall in the lunch room, looking at her thumb nail, biting off a little piece.

"Uh, Miss Barber? I must have someone

43

else's lunch. This one has a candy bar, and I know I wouldn't have a candy bar in mine."

Miss Barber's mouth puckers and she gets that "is this important?" cock to her eyebrow. But she waves it up over her head and yells "Attention, people! Is this someone's candy bar?" Billy and Joe look like they wish it was theirs, but they don't raise their hands. Miss Parker puts the candy bar up on the cafeteria counter and tip-taps off in her spiky shoes. And there it rests, all that creamy chocolate and gooey insides wasting away. I want it so bad. Judy says she bets the cranky cafeteria lady swipes it after we're gone.

Monday in the third grade means a bunch of homework, and I'm doing it when Mother comes home from her job. Seeing Mother makes me smile and smile, inside and out. She hangs up her sweater on the hook behind the door and bends her neck to get the apron over her head. She pulls out the heavy iron frying pan from the cupboard and some hamburger from the refrigerator. Cooking noises happen before she turns her head my way. She looks pleased with herself—what Daddy says looks like a cat with a feather in its mouth.

"Hey, Lil," and she has the biggest grin I ever saw when she finally asks "How did you like your candy bar today?"

Mother's Home

The best, best, best thing in the whole world is
when Mother stays home. Last night she came in
the door, letting the screen door slam behind her.
She was plum wore out and looking down in the
mouth. "The cooking and waitressing job down
at Pete's played out," she said. "Pete's 'ol cousin
Maizie decided she wanted to come back to work,
so I'm laid off."

Oh Boy! I wanted to shout, but Mother's
always worried about the money not coming in so
I just shut my lips tight. Nita hugged Mother's
legs, yelling "Yaaay" and Jack did a little jig.
Sometimes I hate being the oldest.

Today we don't have to go to mean ol'
Aunt Hettie's after school. We get to go home
where Mother is making spam and pineapple
slices in the frying pan. Mother is humming and
looks so pretty and spry. I'm thinking about how
Daddy tells everybody, "Lawdy, can't keep your
mother down very long." And guess what?
Pretty soon, Mother gathers all us kids around in
her arms and says, "I saved all my tips from
Pete's, so shoot, let's have a Halloween party!" A
party, a party? At our house? I do shout now and
jump up and down all over the kitchen. Mother

says we get to invite anybody who wants to come. Golleeee.

Mother gets the party ready. She sets her washing tub on the floor, pours in a bucket of water and throws little red apples in it. For bobbing, she says. Then she hangs up her clothesline from one end of the living room to the other and dangles marshmallows down from it on thread from her sewing basket. She explains to us that we'll have a blindfold and then we'll have to try to eat the marshmallow hanging in front of us. We giggle, just thinking about it. We make a jack-o-lantern from a big fat pumpkin from Mrs. Foster's garden next door. Mother says everybody at the party will get to throw walnuts in the open top and we'll see who gets the most. I show Jack and Nita how to braid together orange and black crepe paper strips from the Five and Dime store on Main Street. We hang them all over the living room, racing to see who can string the most.

All the kids we ask to come to the party say yes. Mother hugs up all the kids that come through the door. She says we all will get a prize, even if we don't win at bobbing apples or catching marshmallows in our teeth. We eat cookies with orange Koolaid frosting on them. We have never, ever had so much fun. I know

I'm never going to forget this party my mother made for us with her tip money.

Tonight Daddy comes home late from the shipyards in Alameda, dragging his heels. We haven't seen him for almost two weeks. Mother brings him hot biscuits with gravy and a heap of scrambled eggs. She's excited, talking a mile a minute about the party, pulling out the left over cookies for his dessert. Jack and Nita are talking at the same time, telling about their friends and the games and all of us are laughing and carrying on.

"Daddy, Daddy," I try to butt in with my story. "My best friend Lupe and her brother Ernesto came all the way out from where they live and Ernesto won the bobbing contest!"

Daddy puts down his fork with a piece of egg hanging from it. He looks over at Mother standing at the sink. Mother turns around and dips her hands into the dishwater swishing the soap bubbles around in the frying pan.

"Lil, you mean they came all the way from Meskin town?"

"Yeah, Daddy. They walked all that way."

"Opal," my Daddy says quiet-like to my Mother, "did Meskins come into this house?"

"Now, Lester, they're just children...Lily's friends."

"Friends," he yells out. "They're Meskins!" "Don't ya'll ever bring those brown-skinned hot-pepper eaters in my house ever again, you hear?" Daddy scrapes back his chair and shoves his plate of food away from him. He stomps on back to the bedroom, his back right straight and his hands fisted tight at his sides. Mother dries her hands a long time before she tells Jack and Nita to go to bed too.

"Mother, what's the matter," I whisper.

She unties her apron, hangs it on the hook by the stove, sits down in her chair at the table and motions me into mine. "Your Daddy hates Meskins. Guess he always will."

"But, why, Mother?"

"Oh, Lil," Mother sighs. "They're different. Different from us. Us Texans."

"But, Mother, Lupe and Ernesto are fun and nice and polite, like you tell us to be. They don't fight. They don't use swear words. They go to church. How could Daddy hate them?"

"They don't go to our church. They come from Mexico. They talk Meskin. Your Daddy and all his kinfolk say they don't belong here."

"Mother, do you like them?"

She looks at her fingernails, twists her little wedding ring circle round and round and smoothes her hair behind her ears. Then she looks up at me and heaves a big breath. "I do like

48

them, Lil. But I'm the only one in our whole family. Except for you. You and me. I guess that makes us sort of different too, huh?"

I'm thinking on this and feeling mighty down and blue.

"And Lily, best not tell your father. No need riling him up, especially when he's so tired. Come on, let's finish this cleanup now. I've got to go find me another job tomorrow."

When I say my prayers tonight I put in a God bless for Meskins and then, I know it's wrong, but I ask God to fix it so there are no jobs out there for Mother to find tomorrow.

Ol' Boots

His sad eyes are begging at me through the screen door. I push the door open. It slaps right smart behind me when I run out and stoop down to him. I remember to hold out my hand, inside up, like Mother says to do when a dog is a stranger. All skinny and wobbling to one side, tail hiding under him, he's sure a sorry sight. His tongue stretches out from under his long black nose and licks my hand all over. He sure stinks. Bad as the hog pen, back on the farm in Texas.

I keep watching over my shoulder to make sure he's still there while I run into the garage. I find an old tuna can in back under the spider webs and scoop some cat food out of the bag on the shelf. Lordy, after he takes two big chomps, it's all gone, and then he scoots that ol' can up against the fence so he can lick round and round inside of it. After he laps up about a gallon of water, his long-haired tail starts to lift up just a little.

Jack comes wheeling up the driveway on his bike. Nita is sitting on the handle bars, all wobbly like. "Hey, dog! What a dirty ol' hound," Jack says, laughing at him.

Nita untangles her legs from the bike and runs over to hug his dirt-stiff neck. She squeals—

squinty, smiley eyes looking up at me, "Is he ours?"

In a little while, when we get brave enough to ask her, Mother says no. "He's maybe lost from his family. Just don't feed him any more and he'll go on home. Leave him be, now."

All day 'til dark Nita and I keep running to the window to see if he's gone. Nope, still there, curled up as close as he can to the front door. At bedtime after we kids say, "I pray the Lord my soul to take," and before the God bless so and so part, I tell Nita and Jack we gotta ask God to bless that sad dirty mutt and help him find his family. Nita butts in, the little pip-squeak. "What's a mutt?"

"Well, if you have to know, right now in the middle of praying time...Daddy says it's a mixed-up dog—some collie dog, some shepherd dog and who-all-knows what else kind-a-dog. Okay, now all together, let's do the God blesses. Start with Mother and Daddy."

Well, you know what? That mutt does find his family. It's us. Daddy and Mother never do say yes. They just give up when we name him Boots, wash him with the hose in the back yard and sneak him table scraps after supper.

Boots likes his home with us, but he likes to travel around too. Sometimes he's gone a day or two and then comes straggling back. Most times, when he wanders on in, he's all beat up looking. One time his ears are chewed, there's dried up blood on his back and he's limping some too. Funny thing though, he struts on up the street headed for our house with his shaggy tail flying in the air like a flag. And something like a smile on his face.

Ol' Boots has a favorite trip. He especially likes to go to the County Fair that comes to our town every summer. It's a sizzling hot day and it's so still you can hear the Ferris Wheel music piping out from the fairgrounds and even the race track betters screaming for their horses. Mother makes us a big pitcher of lime Koolaid, and we're sipping it through stripey colored straws, the kind with a part that bends so you can lay down and suck. Usually, we only get to use these kinds of straws when we're sick in bed, but Mother says they sure come in handy today. "See, children, it's the coolest laying down flat on the porch. Go ahead, just try it." Mother's out here with us, relaxing in her rocking chair. She says,"The Lord meant for us to rest a spell, now and then."

We hear a car coming round the corner. It's Deputy Delgado pulling up in his shiny black cop car in front of our house. Mother turns white, and we all run out to the curb. Deputy Delgado is still trying to push hisself and his big ol' belly out of the car when we get there. In the back seat is Boots, sitting with his head up high, his ears perked pointy-straight and his tongue panting drops of slobber. And something like a smile on his face.

The deputy pulls Boots out of the car with a rope tied round his neck. He wipes the dripping sweat off his shiny head with his red cowboy kerchief and pokes his finger at Mother. "This here pesky dog's been down at the racetrack chasing the horses, high tailing it as fast as they are. Officials had to stop the race… right in the dad-ratted middle. Folks're cussin' mad. This is big trouble I'm telling you. Keep - this - dog - tied - up…(he jerks the rope tight between every word) or else we put him down. You hear me, ma'am?"

We hear him, all right. Soon as Daddy gets home, he finds a rope, ties one end real tight to the fence in the back yard and the other end round Boots' neck. Bootsie hates it. He pulls and squirms and whines and won't eat. But he does chew. Right through the rope.

Next day, Deputy Delgado calls on the telephone and makes us come and get Boots at the race track. He doesn't want blood all over his back seat, he says. We go down there to the track. A little jockey man in a shiny yellow shirt points over to a horse stall where Bootsie is. His back leg is all crumpled up and oozing blood and his tail is laying flat out in the dirt. And he's real still. Mother hugs Nita when she starts to cry.

But when it's all said and done with, Deputy Delgado doesn't make us put him down like he said he would. He figures Boots wouldn't be doing much running anymore after getting kicked so bad. The Deputy doesn't jab his finger at us this time, either, and when he tells how Boots ran faster than the lead horse on the track that day that big ol' cop gets a little shine in his eyes. And something like a smile on his face.

A Bargain Deal

Sick—those two are always getting sick, seems like. Jack's got hurting ears. Nita's got a sore throat. Mother's got a thermometer sticking in their mouths. Finally, the other day, when she takes them back again to Doc Shanks, she asks him, "Well, Doc, what are we going to do about this? These kids are missing way too much school. And, to boot, I'm in big trouble if I have to take off work many more days."

Doc Shanks sits on the corner of his desk, with his long, lanky legs swinging a little and then he drawls out, "It's all about tonsils and adenoids, adenoids and tonsils...yep, that's the problem, all right. What to do about it? Yank 'em out."

Jack and Nita look up at Mother, real bug-eyed like. "Lily, you take the kids outside for a spell. You can play on the sidewalk 'til I'm finished here. Go on now."

Jack and Nita don't feel like playing anything, so we just sit on the steps in front of the Doctor's office, elbows on our knees and hands holding up our chins. "What does that mean, 'yank 'em out', " Nita asks, starting to bring her thumb up to her mouth, forgetting she swore off it a couple of weeks ago.

"Well, I don't know exactly, but probably

Doc Shanks is going to cut 'em out with a little knife, or something like that." That was stupid, I tell myself. Because now Nita starts to bawl— and nobody bawls louder and longer than she does. Jack doesn't look good either, but he knows boys don't cry–least not out on Main Street.

Mother's not going to answer any questions 'til we get home. I don't have any questions because I'm not sick. All the relatives say I got the good health from Daddy's side of the family. "Strong as a horse," they always say. And then they laugh and slap their legs and say "and stubborn as a mule. Too ornery to get sick." Lucky me.

We're sitting round the kitchen table, and Mother gives us Oreos, three each, on a napkin and a glass of milk. We NEVER get sweets in the afternoon, so this news she's about to tell isn't going to be good for Nita and Jack. I'm hoping maybe they'll be so worried they won't be able to eat, and I'll get their cookies.

"Now kids, this won't be too bad. Doc Shanks says he's going to fix it so you won't have sore throats and hurting ears anymore. That's good, huh? So...ya'll are going to the hospital over in Livermore, and he'll take out your tonsils, back there in your throat and your adenoids, somewhere up by your nose. That's where the problem is. Ya'll won't even know when he does it though because you'll be asleep. And, listen to this. Your throat might hurt a little while after the operation, so you kids are gonna get to eat cool, soft things like ice cream and milkshakes and popsicles…all you want. How about that?" Nita and Jack look at each other and start to giggle behind their hands. Shoot, dang! They're even starting to unscrew their Oreos.

Jack and me, we scrape off the white stuff with our teeth. Jack scrapes up and I scrape down. Nita licks it off with her tongue. She's still licking when we crunch up our cookie pieces and slurp them down with some good ol' cold milk. Mmm. Mmm.

"And Lily, you get to do it too!" Mother is looking at me, with her lips curving up at the corners, making little dimples in her cheeks.

What? Gee. I'm thinking Mother doesn't want to play favorites, you know, so I'm going to get ice cream too. How good can this get?

Mother has some more to say. "So next Wednesday I'm taking ya'll to the hospital and checking ya'll in. The Doc says they'll take out the tonsils and adenoids in the afternoon. You're gonna sleep at the hospital all night and I'll pick you up the next morning. Won't that be a funny thing for Daddy and me to be here without you kids? We won't know what to do with ourselves."

Jack's raising his eye brows at me over the top of his glass.

"Moth…errr!!," I scream. "What do you mean…you kids? Not me! I'll be here."

She's fiddling with the edge of a napkin. Uh oh. "I will, won't I?"

Mother folds the napkin with a press of her fingers. "Well, no, Lil. Dr. Shanks says we might as well do all three of ya'll at the same time. He figures you're gonna have tonsillitis one of these days too, so let's get it all over with. And besides he'll give us a bargain deal this way.

The operation day comes, ready or not. It's all white in here. The walls, the linoleum on the floor, the sheets on the three beds all lined up in a row. Well, it's really only two beds now. The nurses, dressed up in white too, wheeled Nita out a while ago, and it's just Jack and me, laid out right straight and tight under the starchy sheets. Mother's here, too. She's sitting in a chair next to Jack, because he's going to be next. Since I'm the oldest I have to be last. She's patting his hand, talking about all the ice cream he's going to eat, soon as it's over.

The white door swings wide open and the white nurses wheel white Nita back in. Yep, she's asleep all right…I think. She's mighty still, her eyes are closed and her long curly hair is

60

streaming out on the white pillow. But there's bright red on that white pillow, too. "Blood!" I scream. "Mother, there's blood dribbling out of Nita's mouth. Mother! Is she dying?"

"Shhh, Lily. You need to be quiet in here. No, she's all right. Just lay yourself back down and rest. They're taking Jack now. Your turn is coming before too long."

She's wrong. Too long comes—way before Jack gets wheeled back in. I watch. He's not moving either and whiter than everything else in here. He's dead, for sure. I know it. And I'm next. My heart starts to thump, thump, thump in my chest and little tears start to leak, leak, leak down my face.

"Mother, this isn't faaa-ir! I'm not siii-ck. Everybody knows I'm too ornery to ever get sick." And I don't care if I'm screaming real loud in this white-quiet place. And I'm going to kick, too…kick off this tight-white sheet and jump off this steel-white bed and run out that slick-white door. I'll show them how ornery I am! Mother shushes and pats and big white nurse hands hold me down, all the way out that door.

The ice cream is white too. But, nobody ever told us we are going to be way too sick to eat it. Liars. A big fat lie—the only thing that is not white.

Fish Fry

Jack sticks his head inside the kitchen door to yell it out, "Wanna jump the creek?" I throw my book on the table.

"Yeah, I wanna. What about Nita?" Jack peeks into the kitchen where Mother's washing dishes and Nita's playing with her dolls on the floor. He says real soft like, "Make her stay home. She's too little to jump the big places, and she'll whine for us to carry her."

Nita hears him anyway. "I am not so. NOT too little!" She's screaming right behind me.

Boy, Nita can really scream too. That time we all got our tonsils out, she fussed and sniveled til Jack got sick of it and beaned her on the head. She screamed so loud that she him-o-ridged. That means her tonsil stitch blew out and blood squirted all over everything...her pajamas and the sheets and the bowl of ice cream. Had to call Doc Shanks and carry her to the hospital.

I'm remembering that time for a little bit. "Uhh...better take her with us Jack. Mother'll make us anyway." But I whisper in his ear, "Boy, is she spoiled." We're ready to go, and Mother says to come on home when she gives the usual signal. It's a yellow dishcloth she pins up on the clothesline. "So, better be looking, every once in a while," she says.

In the big pasture behind our house is the creek. It dries up in the summer, but now it's tumbling and pushing all that rain water from the winter into a long, curvy path all the way to the big draining ditch down below the fence. The weeds up on the banks are real green now and slippery with little yellow flowers popping out on the tall sour grass.

Here's how you play jump the creek: everybody runs real fast along one side of the water …can't stop. And then if you're the leader you quick jump over to the other side when you think you can make it. If you do make it, the kids behind you have to jump too. But, if you slip into the creek, somebody else gets to be leader. Then, you keep moving on up the creek, 'til you get to the silo way up on the far pasture. If you've got Nita with you though, like today, you never make it to the silo because you're too tired lifting her rock hard little body across—every single time.

So, we quit and sit on a big rock watching little polliwogs squiggling around in a puddle. We're thinking what to play next. "I know…let's have a picnic. Let's round up the stuff. Nita, you go beg Mother for a pack of Koolaid and maybe some crackers or something. Jack, you can find

64

some big, flat leaves for plates. I'll get some tin cans from the garage and maybe something for dessert."

Then, I get the best idea of all. "Hey, we could have a fish fry!" Jack wants to know how and Nita whines "I ha-a-a-te fish."

"Lets scoop up some polliwogs and lay them out on a board in the sun...to fry." Jack and Nita just sit there, squinting their eyes up at me. "Come on, it'll be fun...not just play like. It'll be for real." I smile big at them. Come on!"

Well, not so easy snatching up those squirmy little slimies, but we get two each and lay them out on a board by the rock. They're sure wiggling a long time. I'm beginning to feel a little funny in my stomach. "Come on, let's get our other stuff while they're cooking."

The dang little things are still moving some when we get back. I don't like looking at them and the funny feeling is worse, so we start our picnic without fish. I tell Jack to lay out the big leaves on a board from the scrap heap. I scoop up some creek water in the tin cans, put a little pinch of Koolaid in each one and stir it with my finger. Nita says "one for you, one for me, one for you," until the crackers are divided up on the leaves. We eat and drink, making slurp noises with the Koolaid. Dessert was going to be a few mints I saved in my underwear drawer from

Christmas, but I decide I don't want to give them up after all. So I bring three little rocks with just enough dirt on them to suck for awhile. Then, Jack fishes in his pocket and brings out skinny little pieces of sheetrock and a box of matches he found under the house. "Let's have a smoke," he says and scratches a match on a rock. We all try to light up, but finally we have to just play-like smoking because, you know what? No matter what you do, sheetrock won't light.

We're all too full for the fish fry, we say. Good thing. The polliwogs are dead...bad dead. Shriveled. Looking like rat poops. I feel all weak and shaky and something hurts... a lot...inside. I think it's in the middle of my heart. No amount of running around gets rid of it. Chewing sour grass doesn't either.

The flapping yellow dish cloth tells us it's time for supper. "Go on in," I tell Jack and Nita. "I'll come in a minute." I can't though. I've got the miseries...like sad and ashamed and worried. I killed those little polliwogs. I did. I made them suffer out there in hot sun. I want to cry, all by myself, so I head to the big ol' Sycamore tree and climb up the fat limbs to the sitting spot. I make prayer hands and look up in the sky for the God place. "I'm so sorry little polliwogs. I'm praying you swim and squiggle to heaven." I cry and snuffle until almost dark. Mother yells up, "Lily, you come down here, right now, you hear?"

Mother's sitting, waiting for me down there in the grass when I come sliding down the last part of the trunk, my skirt bunching up behind me. She hugs me in her lap, even when she knows I'm way too big. I tell her the fish story, trying not to blubber.

"Lily, that kind of hurting...well, it's called guilt and it's one thing Bayer aspirin won't help. I'm thinking that knowing the name of this sick feeling doesn't help either. When she says guilt can be a good thing, I know she's just trying to make me feel better. I don't.

"But, Lil, see…because it makes you feel so bad, it might keep you from doing something like …a polliwog murder… again."

I used to think nasty, gaggy Castor Oil was the worst thing in the world to swallow, but I just now change my mind. The real worst medicine of all is that guilt thing.

Hear the Train Blow

Down in the valley, valley so low, hear the train whistle, hear the train blow.

I love that song Daddy sings and plays on his Jew's harp, except they call it harmonica in California. And I love the train that whistles and blows, especially at sleeping time—night time rumbling and clackety-clacking on its shiny tracks right across the road from our house. Real good snoozing music it is. Mostly it's moving on through to someplace else, but sometimes it screeches its wheels to a way drawn out stop. Daddy says maybe it's taking sand or something from Kaiser's gravel pit, where uncle Ben works. Or could be just resting a bit before grinding out again in the morning.

This time it brings *us* something. There's a knocking on the back screen door, and Mother yells at me to go see who's there. I can tell it's a man, a man I don't know, standing there with a floppy, greasy hat in his hands, shuffling his fingers round and round it. "Little ma'am," he says to me, ducking his head some, "Could you fetch your mama?"

Mother motions me back and opens the screen door a little ways and peeks out, asking him, "What do you want?"

"I'm real hungry ma'am. I been on the road a long time—no water and nothing to eat. Could you spare me something from your kitchen? I can work, do some chores to pay you."

I can tell by Mother's back and Mother's hands fiddling with her apron that she's thinking a spell. "Well," she finally says, her breath sighing out like she's been holding it, "guess I can rustle up something. You just wait here on the steps, hear?"

"Mother, Mother, who is that man?" I'm whispering low and trailing her into the house.

"Lil, just shush up a minute while I think what to make for him. Lordy, there's not much. Not much we can afford to give away. Guess I can fry up an egg and make a sandwich with those two heels left in the bread box. Run get some salad dressing from the icebox, Lily, and a clean tin can over there on the shelf." Mother's fast, real fast at cooking, so in just a few minutes she takes that slimy, egg smelly meal out to him, along with some warmed up coffee in the tin cup.

"Here mister, it's not much. Go sit on the curb out front to eat it. You can have all the water you want from the hose next to the house. And don't worry yourself about working any."

I watch him from the window stuff that sandwich, in big pieces, into his cheeks, a drool of

70

egg yellow running down his chin. He drinks the coffee in one big swallow and heads to the hose.

"Lily, come away from there. You don't need to be staring at the poor thing. I swear he must be starving."

"He's a hobo," Mother tells me when I pester her about it again. "He doesn't have a home, so he rides the train. I guess he's hoping to find work somewhere. So many of them nowadays…breaks your heart. But Lily, you dare not tell your Daddy about this, about me feeding him because he won't like it one bit."

"But why, Mother?"

"Lordy, Lord Lily, will you ever stop asking why?" Mother rubs her hand over her forehead and looks me in the eyes. "The why is, if you just have to know everything, Daddy says we don't hardly have enough money to feed ourselves, let alone the tramps. Go along now and don't ask me anymore about it, you hear?"

I open the top drawer of the dresser in the little bedroom where Nita and I sleep. Have to be quiet like. I reach in the way back, behind Nita's underclothes and socks. It's still there. Of course, it's still there, I'm thinking. Nita keeps her sweets forever, pulling out one, now and then, from her hiding place to lick or chew or suck it in front of Jack and me, looking smirky, because she knows we eat ours up soon as we get them. It's a pretty red shiny box Mrs. Berger, from across the way, gave her last Christmas with two layers of candy, a crinkly white tissue paper between them. There's still some candy sitting there on the top layer, a chewy one and three peppermint sucking pieces. I lift up the tissue and slide my hand under it to find what's left there on the bottom of the box. Fingers searching, searching. Durn. I must of stole all those already and forgot about it, or Jack's been in here too. I know Nita's going to find out and go running to Mother, and I'll get a big talking to, but I pull out the last chewy and two of the peppermints anyway, close the top and shove the box into the back again.

The hobo man is across the road now, leaning against the big leafy tree next to the tracks. I look for cars, this way, that away and run over there. Ooo-whee. He smells like a garbage can. It's real bad. And his clothes are crusty dirty. His shoes have soles that flap up and down with holes on the bottom. No shoe laces. No socks neither. "Mister hobo," I kind of whisper like. He looks up at me from under his stained, rusty looking hat. "Here, here's some sweets. They're real good. You'll like them." I drop the candies into the smudgy-sooty looking hand he holds out to me.

His eyes are watery. "Thank ye, little ma'am. I shore appreciate it." He nods and nods his head and picks out a pink peppermint to slip into his mouth. He closes his eyes. He sings, mmm, mmm, mmm.

Mister hobo man is gone the next morning when I look out. But I can hear, way down in our valley, the train that whistles and blows. Bet you he's on it.

Summer Feet

Boy howdy, it's a hot ol' summer day in Texas. It's our every other summer visit back to the family. Jack and me are sitting up on the hill behind Aunt Dorothy's house, our bare feet sticking out in the dust. "Lemme see yours." I poke at the soles of Jack's grimy feet. "Yeah, but look at mine. Mine are so tough I could climb sharp rocks up a mountain. Betcha I could even walk on flamin' hot rocks, my feet are so tough."

"Naah, you can't," Jack says. "Besides, where you gonna get flamin' rocks?"

"Betcha anyway."

Jack starts to argue back, but a big ol' bunch of dust flies up behind us.

It's the cousins. The mean ones. Wilber and Clyde screeching up the hill on their bikes, stopping real close to our backs. Heard tell from Granpa what devils they are. "Why one time," he said," Preacher Dale was coming to Sunday dinner at their house and those little dickens strung up a wire through the bushes on the path so he'd trip and fall down. And he did! He couldn't even preach the next Sunday. I bet they got big whuppins for that one. 'Nother time, they stole Aunt Maybelle's wig right off her dresser when she was sleeping. She had to go round bald-headed for a week before they found it in the chicken coup—two eggs in it."

"Hey, what ya'll doing?" Wilber yells real loud when he slides off his old bike and drops it in the dirt.

"Nuthin'," Jack says, squinting up at him. I can tell he's afraid, but he doesn't want to show it. Clyde rides his bike around in slanty circles, spewing up dust, showing off and spitting down at our feet when he puts on his brakes in front of us.

"Hey, Jack, wanna race down the hill? You can use Wilber's ol' heap."

"I dunno. That bike looks too big for me," his voice is kind of wavery like.

"You little sissy. You're just afraid I'll beat you."

"Nuh-uh!" Jack screams back, all red in the face. Oh, Jack, I'm thinking, whatever you do— don't cry. Your life won't be worth a plug nickel.

"I'll race you," and I stand up to show him I mean it.

"I'm not racing no girl." He snorts and cuts his eyes at Wilber.

"You're the sissy then, Clyde," I yell in his face.

"Okay, but you're asking for it," and he goes over to get Wilber's bike. He shoves it at me, and I climb up on the beat up ol' thing. But it's hard because there's no rubber on the pedals and my dusty feet keep sliding off. I have to get off and spit on my hands and try to clean off the bottom of my feet. Then I figure out how to clamp my toes around the steel posts of the pedals.

We line up at the top of the hill. Wilber yells out, "Get on your marks. Get set. Go!" I push off, pedaling as fast as I can. It's real bumpy going down and steeper than I thought. Oh Lord, I'm flying! And my heart is going like a jack-hammer. About half way down, the front wheel hits a rock, and I go ever-which-a-way. Got to hang on to the handle bars tight, tight and clinch my toes harder, harder on those steely posts. Whoo-ee. Lordy, Lord, I'm about to crash!

At the bottom of the hill, all tangled up in the bike, I can't breathe, telling you, not one breath. My wind is plum sucked out of me. "H-E - L- P!" I want to scream, but nothing comes out of my mouth. I can hear Jack crying, running down the hill, yelling for Mother. Clyde and Wilber, the rats, are running lickety-split the other way.

My foot hurts. . .so bad. I twist around to look at it. I'm about to vomit. That steel pedal post is stuck right into the bottom of my foot.

Maybe clean through. In the soft part, in the middle place between the hard, tough, summer soles. Mother comes running, fast, right now, grabs that steel rod and pulls that thing out. Just like when she pulled the scissors out of Jack's forehead—the time when he forgot about the running rule.

"A dough poultice is what it needs," Aunt Dorothy says that night. We're staying with Mother's family, and everybody in town comes in to say their piece about the hole in my foot. I wear that mooshy mess made with flour and water and hot mustard stuff on my foot for three days, but I still can't walk and swallowing down aspirins won't take the hurt away. Mother says we better take me to the doctor. We have to borrow money from all the relatives and even the neighbors so we can do it.

I have a white cast on my foot, and it goes all the way up my leg to my knee. It doesn't hurt anymore, but it's so itchy under there that Mother got me a long, skinny stick to scratch with. I get crutches, and Jack and Nita are so jealous. But now it's time to go back to California, and Mother is worried about how I'll get onto the train to go home.

It's a troop train, because it's wartime, and we ride with the soldiers going and coming. All of us, standing down by the tracks, trying to figure out how I'm going to get up all those steps to the train car and then down again and up again every blamed time we have to change trains. My mother used to chop wood, walk six miles to the store, and haul a long sack of cotton and now she tries real hard, but she just can't lift me and my heavy cast up those stairs.

A tall soldier walks over our way. My pretty mother smiles at him, and he smiles back. I get swooshed up, crutches and all and carried up those stairs and down that aisle to our seats. Sergeant Johnny is his name, and he is our friend all the way home.

My tough ol' summer feet don't last all the way to Thanksgiving this year, but one of them has a purpley, half-moon scar that'll last forever. Can't wait to show it off to Wilber and Clyde, next summer visit. My Daddy says those two durn devils will be green with envy…whatever that means.

Fitting In

My paper dolls have so many clothes that sometimes a few hang out from under the squished down lid of the old shoebox. Whenever I get a new set, I clip them out with Mother's finger nail scissors, going around the lines so careful like, especially so I don't, on accident, cut off any of the little tabs that hold the dresses on the dolls. Everyday dresses, flouncy party dresses, long, trailing dance dresses and play-outside dresses . Even go-to-church dress-up with gloves and hats. This is the very best play-like-pretend of all, deciding what my paper dolls should wear.

I have two real dresses of my own. One is blue flowered, little petals sprinkled all over. The other one is green with orange and white sunflowers. Mother makes them on her sewing machine with material from big used-up flour sacks. They both have puffy short sleeves, three buttons down the front and a sash to tie around your middle. Mother peddles fast and steers the cloth around the needle, leaning this way and that way making it go where she wants it to. She zips to the end and bites off the loose thread. Mother's hands are little with stubby fingers and clipped–off-short finger nails. Everything she does with them is quick and strong. If I'm careful, I can wear one dress for two days and then switch to the other one, so Mother can wash and starch and iron the first one, so as to be ready for its turn. The other girls at school don't have to do the switching and washing thing.

But, guess what happened today! My heart is beating so fast I can hardly tell you about it. Now, I have three dresses. I just got the most bee-u-tee-ful new dress in the whole world! Well, not exactly new, but it looks like it. Slippery, slidey store-bought material, so white and shiny it hurts your eyes some to stare at it. And just look at the pleats, lots of them on the skirt and two rows of golden buttons, marching from the waist right up to the collar. Puts me in mind of a parade.

"Gollleee! Mother, Mother, it's the purt …prettiest thing I ever saw. Where did it come from?" She pert-near can't tell me for grinning so big.

"Mrs. Turner, from work, she sent it. Her little girl grew out of it."

"Can I wear it to school tomorrow, can I, can I? Please, Please?" Two little wrinkles show up between Mother's eyes. I just know she's going to say no.

"Hmmm...well, I reckon, one time," she says instead. "Just be specially careful not to get it dirty. It's for dress-up, you know."

Tomorrow brings rain and puddles and mud. But I can do it. I walk backwards, figuring I'll go slow and careful that way. I pick up my feet in my red-rubber boots and set them down, quiet like, trying to get around the squishy, splashy stuff on the dirt path to school. I keep my eyes right where I'm going and right on my snow-white dress. I can't wait to show Judy and Patty and the stuck up girls that say I don't fit in with them and Miss Barber and...

NO!! Lord-a-mercy, here comes Bootsie, loping, sploshing along, tongue slopping out, trying to catch up with me. "Boots, go home! Nooo, down, down!" Two streaks of paw-mud slide right down the front of me, making black trails between the row of my marching band buttons. Tears and swiping and scrubbing with my knuckles don't help a thing. Can't be late. Can't go home. Can't just stand here.

I am late though when I get to school, but Judy and Patty and Miss Barber fuss over me, say the dress is beautiful anyway, say it will wash out, say come on, don't cry anymore.

Patty whispers to me, "Wanna play after school today? On the playground?" I think she asks me because she feels sorry for me, for my bad day with my new dress. Mostly she sides with the stuck up bunch, leaving me out. But I don't care why this time. I do want to play.

When the bell rings I find Jack waiting for me outside, kicking some gravel around. "Hey, Jack. You go on. Tell Aunt Hettie I'm playing at school for awhile, okay?" That hateful woman's taking care of us again cuz Mother has to work. Boy Howdy! I'm so glad I don't have to go home yet. Jack looks mean at me and spits in the dirt before he hangs his head and stomps off.

We scrape the dirt and gravel off a spot on the concrete sidewalk, shake the jacks and ball out of Patty's velvety drawstring bag and make a diamond with our legs spread out, shoes touching at the heels. Tossing the ball, scooping the jacks: onesies, twosies, threesies. I make it all the way to tensies before I miss. Patty sort of smiles. "You're pretty good," she says. But, I worry she might be jealous and might not play anymore. So I say, "Let's go swing on the bars, okay?"

Just when we're getting all hot and sweaty, a lady opens the lunch room door and yells out, "Time for refreshments." Gee. For us? I look at Patty. She's not looking at me, shuffling her shoes around in the dirt. After a little bit, she takes off running and yells over her shoulder "Come on." We race to the open door.

One of the long cafeteria tables has a lacey cloth on it and a teapot and a big bowl full of red punch, with little orange slices floating round in it. Cookies with pink and yellow sprinkles on them and little fluffy cupcakes are all laid out on a doily sitting on a round glass plate. Ladies are standing round in little bunches, talking and smiling. Kids are lining up at the table. One of the ladies, in a purple party dress, comes over to me waiting behind the other kids in line. "Hello young lady. What's your name?" I tell her in my best polite voice. "Hmmm," she says, with her pointer finger on her chin. "Well, Lily, who is your mother? Is she here?"

"Well, no ma'am. She's at work."

"Oh. I see." The lady's voice sounds like it's trying to make up its mind. "Well, I'm sorry deary, but this meeting is for the Ladies Club, and I'm afraid your mother isn't a member. Better run along home...or where ever you go after school." Her hand reaches around to the back of my white Bootsie-muddied-up dress, turning me, steering me to the lunch room door. It closes big and heavy behind me. Slam!

Patty in. Me out.

Out. Outside...of the others who belong ...the others who all fit in.

Songs in the Cold and the Dark

My warm feet, just out of bed, hate touching the icey linoleum on the floor. It's freezing and black at 4:30 on this winter morning. For sure, it is as cold as a well-digger's butt. I better not say that out-loud. Nita will squeal on me if she hears it. It's not fair though. Daddy says it all the time. It's the butt part. Mother says butt is a bad word. "Butt, Butt, Butt, Butt," I whisper while I run my fingers along the wall to find the closet. I feel around in there and pull out my blue jeans, a sweater, a fat jacket, a scratchy wool cap, and some red mittens, one with a hole in the thumb.

Better tip-toe out the door without squeaking the floor. Nobody else in the house is ready to wake up yet. I have to feel my way through the living room to get a flashlight and my boots. Well, here's the tree, a branch tickling my arm. All the packages are piled around. The flashlight shows me a bike for Jack and a golden haired baby doll for Nita that Santa Claus brought. Huh...Santa Claus. What Santa Claus?

Talk about not fair! Not right! Liars! That's what they are—Mother and Daddy. Big ol' terrible liars. I remember how I argued with everybody that day at school. I told them all, "Nuh-uh! There is so too a Santa Claus." And they sniggered and giggled and pointed their fingers at me, elbowing each other in the ribs. "I know there's a Santa Claus. Everyone in my family and my aunts and uncles and a bunch of cousins and even Mrs. Parks, she knows everything. They all know there's a Santa Claus." I screamed and gritted my teeth so I couldn't cry. "My family doesn't lie, you know!"

Well, it turns out they do. Mother finally tells me the truth when I cry about what the kids said at school. I can't believe it. I cry again and throw myself around on the couch and yell at her. "Liars! You and Daddy. I'll never trust you again." And you know the worst of it? She tells me I have to lie too. "Lily, so the magic won't be spoiled for Jack and Nita," she says, not quite looking at me. I'm still mad, come to think of it, and I kick my boots up against the closet wall. Wake 'em up? I don't care!

I make it out of the house into the still-starry morning and run down the street to the church. Under the street light, they're gathering, our little choir, steam puffing out of their cheeks and a few flashlight beams streaking through the dark. Got here just in time. Mr. Tripp, his white hair fringing out from under a fuzzy green cap, huddles us all together, and we start down Second Street, shivering and hugging ourselves. For real, Daddy, well-digger's butt. Butt. Butt. Old Mr.

Krueger's house is first on the block. Mr. Tripp raises his hand, and we all hum a little first—warming up our pipes, he says. "Okay, all together singers, Silent Night."

I'm not a musician. Oh sure, Mother makes me take piano lessons, but I can't just sit down, like Cousin Wanda, and play anything somebody shouts out. Daddy says he's throwing all of that money for lessons right down a rabbit hole. But Texans, especially my family, can do two things really good, just naturally. That's telling stories and singing. And I can sing—sure can.

In the cold, in the dark, this Christmas morning, all of us sing those sweet, pure notes... so beautiful they catch up my breath. This is just right, just right. Mother, this is the real magic. And nobody has to lie.

After making folks smile all up and down the town, Mrs. Tripp, in her cute little Elf cap, hands out big coffee cups full of hot chocolate with marshmallows floating in the foam. The sun squeezes through the leaves of the oak trees and we yell "Merry Christmas" over our shoulders, heading for home.

Daddy opens the door for me, turkey smells beginning to escape. "I'll be danged, Lily, I don't how in the world you can get up at the crack of dawn and stand out there in the cold—

sangin'! It's so early, it's a wonder you didn't bump into Santa Claus. Right, Nita?"

I figure out that Santa Claus is some kind of thing that folks like lying about and kids like too—until they get told different. And then, danged if they don't do it to their kids too. Well, not me, no sirree, not me. Not ever.

Uncle Sam Wants You!

Our ball is growing bigger and bigger every day. After all the shiny wisps and strips and wads get all smoothed out, I press them together hard with my fingers, to make it round. I like looking at it, up there in its place on my side of the dresser drawers. It's on my side because I'm in charge. Being in charge can be good or bad. But I'm always it because I'm the oldest. Everybody in town saves tinfoil: chewing gum wrappers and the insides of cigarette packs mostly. I make Jack and Nita look in the gutters, in the garbage, out in the horse field, on the floor in the grocery store. Then they get to watch while I take all the little pieces and stick them onto the ball. When it's big enough Mother will take it down to the collection center. We all have to do our part because it's The War.

I love the radio. After the Lone Ranger sings out, "Hi yo Silver, away!" we know it's bedtime. But tonight Mother and Daddy say I can stay up to listen to the Fireside Chat with them. "Hee, hee, hee. I get to stay uh-up," I sing-song-whisper to Nita and Jack when they have to go to bed.

Daddy says FDR is going to talk to us, to tell us about what's happening in The War. I can tell by the way they sit, leaning in toward the radio, that I can't say a word 'til it's over. FDR says we all need to help the war effort. "But why are we fighting, Daddy? When will it be over? Daddy, do you have to go fight? "

Mother and Daddy try to answer all my whiney questions. After awhile, Mother pats me on the back, tells me not to be a worry-wart and waves me off to bed.

The springs creak when I get into the bed with my sister, who's still too little to worry about The War. I'm trying to lie here very still and think of a happy thing to put me to sleep. Christmas morning...that's always a good one. But I can't make the pictures behind my eyes show Daddy's old stockings hanging low, stuffed with oranges and nuts, the candy canes sucked to a sticky point or even the presents ripped open. Instead, I see Daddy in a soldier uniform, socking and punching the Germans who are marching up our driveway, bombs falling on our house from buzzing fighter airplanes. Now Daddy is on a ship that is burning and sinking, the dirty Japs doing it. The newsreel at the Roxie Theatre last Saturday showed how it is...The War. I'm going to pray now that Daddy can stay home and not be a soldier or a sailor, even if Uncle Sam does want him and FDR says so too.

Mother says daddy probably won't have to

go to the war because maybe he's too old and has three little children. But he does go...not to war, but to the shipyards in Alameda and Richmond. He's gone a long time everyday. Sometimes he just sleeps there in his clothes on the deck of the big ship and starts up again when the sun comes up. I haven't seen Daddy for a long time, and I have to be in charge a lot now.

Jack is sitting at the kitchen table this morning drawing with the red and black crayons. He makes "ka-pows" and shrieks and whines with his voice while the black crayon shoots bullets from a dive bombing plane and then the red crayon explodes into flames from the fighter with a swastika on it. Jack is still pretty little too. Maybe this is what he does for the war effort.

The three of us, even little runt Nita, make up games about victory. We draw pictures in the dirt outside the house with sticks from the wood pile. We make Japs and Nazis and then dance around them in a hand-holding circle singing, "Planes over land, ships over sea, the army and navy overtake the enemy!" Then we stomp them and kick them and shovel dirt all over those filthy rats. We never show this game to Mother though. She would shake her finger and tell us, "Don't you be doing that with your shoes! You have to make do with those...for the duration." "The doer- a- shun. It means 'til The

War is over," I tell Jack when he asks me. After the duration, we won't have to use stamps to get gas and meat and shoes and sugar. And we will have peace.

There's all kinds of victory stuff. We're supposed to have a Victory garden, and we sure do, since we come from Texas farming stock. The more we can grow, the more we can eat and give out to others, too. But the Victory stamps and the Victory bonds are what I do for the war effort. My job is licking the defense stamps into the defense books, saving up for a defense bond. But what I do best is sell them. In the fifth grade, they show you how. The way you do it is take the papers and a pencil and the official envelope, walk around the neighborhood, knock on doors and tell people about The War effort and Victory bonds. And they buy them right on the spot!

Down at the Post Office, there are two big posters on the wall next to the mail slot. One is Uncle Sam, in his tall flag colors hat and his long, bony finger pointing right at you. He says "I need your skill in a war job." I'm proud that my Daddy is in a war job. The other poster shows a woman in a scarf, making a fist with her arm in a big muscle. She's Rosie the Riveter. She shoots nails into airplane parts to hold them together. My mother doesn't rivet. But she works at the USO. She makes cookies there and serves them to the army and navy men with hot coffee. She plays checkers and sews on their missing buttons. And she goes to the Red Cross. That's when I'm in charge at home.

In the sixth grade, two big things happen. In April, the Principal calls us all together in the auditorium upstairs at school, everybody, even Mr. Anderson, the janitor and Miss Harris, the secretary and all those wiggly Kindergartners. Mr. Benton shushes us. He stands there a long time waiting 'til nobody is whispering or moving. He looks out at us. I think I can see some tears in his eyes. Sounds like a frog in his throat when he tells us, "President Roosevelt is dead." FDR, my FDR, is dead? What about the war effort? What about fireside chats? FDR can't be dead. The duration isn't over yet.

After the school bell lets us out early, Debbie and Judy and I walk home through the spring-budding streets together, holding hands …worrying together. "But listen—my Dad says Truman is okay and he's smart," Judy tells us. "Maybe we'll all be safe." It sounds like a question when she says it, her voice quivery, holding off a cry. I do cry, trying to sop up the tears with my sleeve. FDR is my President, mine, all eleven years of me. What will we do?

Mr. Benton calls us again to the auditorium. It is May 8th. He tells us it is VE day. Victory over Europe! We hug and jump up and down and scream and tears run down our faces. At the Roxie theatre the newsreels go on and on with the cheering in the streets, the confetti in the air.

We celebrate again when the Victory over Japan happens in August, 1945. I think about my FDR, wishing he could be sitting by the fireside, telling us the good news.

Tonight I write in my diary: The duration is over.

After the War

When the shipyards over in Alameda stop running day and night, Daddy comes home. To stay. One night, all of us around the supper table, Daddy says he's been thinking on what to do now that his wartime job is over. "Working all those hours and your mother working too, we saved up a little money, so I believe I'll just take some time off and learn something new. I might just surprise ya'll."

The surprise is that Daddy heeds that ol' Eddards saying, you know the one: "Wish in one hand and spit in the other and see which one gets full the fastest." He says he just plum got tired of wishing in one hand, so he reckoned he'd go on and sign up for Barber College. Our eyes do bug out awhile when he tells us this. Daddy always did cut kinfolks' hair when they needed it, just to help out, so I guess he figures it's about time to make some money at it.

Daddy drives every day, seems like a long time, into Oakland to the Barber College. At first, every night he brings home a new book to add to the growing stack on the dining room table. After my homework, I help Daddy with his. Oh, he can do the cutting part real easy. He makes 100% every time. The learning part about all the muscles and bones and nerves and skin and hair follicles is a sight harder. I get to test him when he thinks he has it all memorized. And he must have passed everything because one day he brings home that Barber's certificate with the official gold seal, all proper in a shiny black frame. The very next day, he sets out to look for a barbering place to work.

When he finds that place over in Livermore, he buys two white, button-up-the-side barbering uniforms and his black zip-top barbering satchel. What a sight to see. Mother says he is the most handsome man in town.

Well, Daddy works so hard and so good that he makes enough money to buy his own shop, right smack dab on Main Street in leafy-treed Pleasanton. "Got a real barber pole out front and two cuttin' and shavin' chairs, and they both swivel, smooth as can be," he says, puffing out his chest and sticking his thumbs under his suspenders, play acting big and important. "And wait 'til you see those six, soft-seated, waiting-for-your-turn chairs. Pretty durn good, wouldn't ya'll say!"

Mother finds a new job too. Those quick, sturdy little fingers of hers are just the thing for tying fishing flies for Mr. Johnson's business downtown. She even gets to bring her tying board and those beautiful glittery feathers and shiny coils to work on at home. No more Aunt Hettie after school! Praise the Lord.

Preacher Dale, back in Texas, always said that the Lord helped those who helped themselves. Well, sure enough we did.

I reckon that's what Ol' Eddards might of been saying too.

The Compact

The long white sticky strip of adhesive tape (and a few band-aids at the end, because we run out of tape) splits up our bedroom straight down the middle. Nita's side. My side. "Better not step one toe over, or I'll stomp it, do you hear me?" I'm so mad I might strangle her! What a brat.

It's all about Ralph Baker, my dream boat. Who knew I would have a crush on the skinny kid sitting next to me in first grade who tried to teach me how to draw steps on the picture of our school that Miss Olson said to make. Now, Ralph is tall, with wavy black hair and long eye lashes. And he rolls up the sleeves on his white T-shirt just right—you know, little narrow folds. I could die, really die when he looks over at me at recess. No kidding, my heart bangs in my chest and I feel like I might faint on the concrete. Judy giggles and drags me across the school yard to whisper in my ear, her hand cupped and her eyes darting around, making sure the other girls don't hear. "Lily, he is sooo cute! You better make your move pretty quick before Barbara gets him." I'm not sure what a move is, but I'm not going to tell that to Judy—who is "Miss when- your- back-is- turned- tell-it-all-to-anybody."

Next day, I can't believe it when Ralph and I get to sit next to each other in a circle with the other kids that Mr. Harris assigns to plan the eighth grade dance. Ralph pipes up first. "Somebody get a pencil and paper so we can make a list. You know, who's going to do what." Cripes, I'm dying. He's smart, too! Be still heart—somebody might hear you thumping. I figure I better move fast, like Judy says, so I squeek out, "I'll do it, Ralph," and I run over to my desk.

It's going to be in the auditorium, and we'll drape yellow and blue crepe paper streamers along the ceiling and hanging down the walls. We decide on Hawaiian punch and chocolate chip cookies and we'll set them out on the long table by the stage, right next to Harry Barlowe's record player. We'll all bring a stack of records.

Oh Lord. Ralph is touching me on my shoulder. My whole body is full of prickles and tingles. "Lily, what records do you have?" he asks. My mind is gone. I can't think of the name of even one.

"Uh, gosh, you know the usual. What do you have?"

Ralph smiles (dimples...I'm swooning) and says, "Something you'll like I bet. I'll pick out a couple for us to dance to." Noooooo. It can't be! He wants to dance with me at the graduation dance. I will faint, die right now for sure.

Tonight's the night. I'm worrying about my hair and my finger nails and how my teeth stick out in front and the ugly scratch on my leg from one of Nita's thirteen cats. She's such a creep. Honestly, I wish I could turn her in for some other sister. I love my new dress. It's dusty rose, with a dropped waistline and pleats all around. Nobody will know it's a hand-me-down from cousin Neva. She hardly ever wore it, I bet.

While I'm worrying about real problems, Mother is worried I'm…well… sick. Just because I'm coughing a little, she sticks a thermometer in my mouth. She holds it up to the light, squints her eyes and frowns down her eyebrows. "Lily, this is sky high. I bet you've got the flu; it sure is going around. You can't go to a dance sick like this."

There is no way that I am not going to this dance. "Mother, I haaave to. I will die if I don't. You'll have to bury me. Just give me two aspirins and a slug of cough medicine, and I'll be all fixed up in plenty of time before the dance. Oh Mother, please, it's the most important night of my whole life."

Mother stares me down, then rubs her hands over her eyes. "All right, Lily. But if your temperature is still high later on, you do not go. Hear that?" I swallow three aspirins, suck on two two ice cubes, stick my face in the refrigerator, and pray the thermometer won't tell on me.

Mother lets me go.

The dance is heavenly. Ralph asks me to dance seven times, and I think I can die happy when he whispers he likes me and wants to give me a graduation present. Oh, man, this is too good to be true. Maybe I'm dreaming it. I do feel kind of hot and dizzy and weak-kneed like. I forget all about it when he reaches into his jacket pocket and pulls out a little package wrapped in silver paper and tied with a red satiny bow. "This is for you, Lily." Ralph holds out the gift, his eyes on the floor.

I mumble back, "Oh, Ralph, thank you. I'm so surprised. Thank you. Uh, should I unwrap it now?"

Ralph sort of stammers out, "Well, I guess not. It's for graduation night. You can open it then." He fiddles with his jacket sleeve and looks over his shoulder a little bit. "Well, that's what my Mom said to do. Is that okay?" I want to scream, "It's all A-OKAY. It's wonderful! This is the best day of my whole life!" But what I tell him is "sure."

Judy's Dad picks us up after the dance because we're going to stay over at her house for a pajama party with Betty and Pat. Two blocks from Judy's house I remember. "Oh, Mr. Simmons, I'm sorry, I forgot my overnight suitcase at home. Could you…Before I can finish he's doing a U-ee, in the middle of the block, screeching the tires. I climb out of the car and try to run into the house, but my legs are shaky, and I have to practically crawl up the stairs. In our bedroom, Nita is sitting up in bed, curlers in her hair, snuggling three cats. "Got to get my suitcase. Go back to sleep." But first I put the beautiful box from Ralph up on my dresser, and oh-so carefully pet the shiny bow and throw it a kiss.

Mr. Simmons is revving up the engine outside, and we make a flying leap out from the curb. Makes my head all light and swimmy, and I'm so hot I have to open the window. When we get there, he slams the car door and heads for bed. We all file into the kitchen to find something to eat. I'm just about to tell them all about Ralph and the box…and you know, the last thing I remember is thinking, before I hit the floor, "I could just faint."

After Daddy opens our front door and puts out his arms to help me in, and Mr. Simmons swears, stomps out and streaks his car down the street, I take medicine from Mother's hand and stagger down the hall, holding on to the walls. I make it to our divided bedroom. Nita has cheated. She is on my side, standing by my dresser— the silver paper and the red bow and the white box— stacked on top. A glittery gold compact is open in her hands, and when she sees me, her bugged-out eyes are scared to death. I scream. Nita screams. The compact slips out of her hand onto the hardwood floor.

I fall down on my knees and scoop it toward me. The little square glass, a long crack splitting it jaggedly in half, reflects back to me a crumpled and tear-drippy face, broken—to match my heart. I will just die.

Girl-Woman Stuff

I'm smiling all over. It's the last day of school in the eighth grade, recess time, and we're all acting crazy, running around in squiggling, giggling bunches of girls, screaming at anything and nothing. I'm handing around my autograph book and signing a bunch of others. There's a page for every student in the class with each name printed at the top. Everybody gets to write something about each other. I'm reading the page for Mary Lee Meyer, poor pudgy thing. There's one note scrawled in the corner of the page that says "five months." I can't think what that could mean. I'm embarrassed to ask anybody but Judy, and when I do, I wish I hadn't. "Lily, how stupid can you be! That means she's so fat she looks like she's five months pregnant."

Stinging hot, that's what my face feels like when she tells me in that snooty tone of voice. That's a word we are never to say at our house— pregnant. If somebody is, and we have to talk about it somehow, we can call it "in the family way." So, I laugh to show Judy, of course, that I get it. "I was just fooling around with you," I say. But I don't. Get it.

In May when we have our spring band concert in the big upstairs auditorium, and I am blaring real loud on my clarinet in the middle of the "Stars and Stripes Forever" something wet starts sliding down my leg. When the final notes fade away, I have a chance to go to the girls bathroom and check on the weird sticky stuff in my underpants. I see blood splats all over. Huh? Lordy, could you blow a clarinet so hard a blood vessel would pop open? I figure maybe I better switch to the flute.

Later today, when Mother gets home from grocery shopping, I tell her all about the mysterious blood spots. Her face turns pink, and she looks up at the ceiling for awhile. She sighs big. "Well, Lily, that's what happens to girls when they grow up to be women." She decides to say some more with her eyes on her hands. "This is an important step in your life. Why, my goodness, you are a woman now. Wait here a minute, I have to get something for you."

She comes back in, twisting a hank of her hair around her finger, as if it were in need of a good curling. "Here, Lily, read this little pamphlet. It tells all about it." On the shiny cover it says "Modess" in purple print, and when I turn the page, I'm looking at pictures of little pads of cotton that Mother says you wear to catch the blood every time it happens. "But Lily," she adds, "it costs way too much for us to buy those little pads, so let me show you where the bag of clean white rags is." She demonstrates how to rip them in strips and fold them, long ways. Then she hands me two really big safety pins that will hold the folded rag onto my underpants. "And, Lily, remember to scrub out any stains on your underpants with cold water right away. We can't afford a lot of new pairs." Sounds like a whole lot of work and a big mess to me.

"Do boys have to do this too?"

"No, Silly. Of course not. Don't forget to read the book all the way through and then give it back to me so your sister doesn't get into it yet." Mother turns her back and leaves the kitchen. End of the lesson.

Blast it! Am I mad! What a big fat bother! And Jack, the lucky creep, won't have to do this at all. It's not fair! I hate it. I stomp and scream: I DO NOT WANT TO BECOME A WOMAN!!

The next and only other lesson happens in the summer before high school. There are huge posters tacked up all over town telling about a new movie mothers and teen-age daughters need to see. The bright red signs scream out: "UNWED TEEN-AGE MOTHER , A Tragedy No One Wants to Endure!" Underneath the message is a photograph of a sobbing mother clutching a pregnant girl. I am shocked, like ice water poured on your head, when my mother says we will go. The movie ushers won't let girls in without their mothers, and the mother has to sign a paper proving that she wants us to be there.

On the day of the movie, we all line up outside the Roxie Theatre, excitement crackling down the street. There is an ambulance parked in front of the theatre, its red light flashing on and off. There are nurses stationed in the lobby, dressed in stiff, snow white uniforms and razor sharp folded hats. They stand like soldiers on guard beside stretchers and oxygen tanks. The theatre manager announces on a mega phone that these emergency procedures are necessary in the case of fainting, vomiting, or other maladies associated with reactions to the graphic, realistic nature of the film.

The girls are tittering in little groups lined up to enter, deliciously fidgety and nervous. The mothers, with pursed lips and clutched purses, hover near their daughters, waiting for the usher to give the sign to file in. We can't wait for the lights to dim after we settle into our seats. Every girl in town and her mother seem to be there whispering in awe. The movie scares the bejeebies out of me. It tells the horrifying story of a teen-age girl who shames her family, who has to leave school and who, with immense agony, gory bloodiness and unbearable screaming and wailing, gives birth to a poor, fatherless baby.

No one faints or vomits, but we all file out without a sound to each other—numb.

My mother and I do not look at each other on the way home. We do not talk about the movie. Not one word. The message is clear. And terrifying. But I still don't know how all of this pregnancy crime comes to be. How can I possibly avoid shame, pain, and disgrace without knowing how it happens?

In the summer I spend long hours at the library, sneaking time in the "S" stacks looking for books that have "sex" in the title. I need to be careful, though, to wander and browse in other sections too, like History and Biography, so Miss Librarian won't suspect what I am up to. And worse yet, tell Mother!

The Toni

I need a Toni. No, I've *got* to have a Toni. Judy and Pat and Charlotte all have Tonies. I hope it's not too late, because the Freshman dance is tomorrow night. I better hurry; the drug store is going to close real quick.

"Motherrrr. Mother!" Jeez, she's on the phone. Waving in front of her eyes doesn't do it. A note, yeh, a note. Can't find a pencil. Shoot! Okay, here it is. I scribble real fast. " Mother, please get off the phone. I have to talk to you...now."

I shove it into her hand and stare right at her, my eyes saying "please, please," my hands in the prayer pose. Oh good, I think she's beginning to wind down the conversation. "Well, Angie, I guess I better get off the phone now. Lily's having a fit about something."

"What is it Lily that couldn't wait just a minute?" She's got her fists on her hips. I better talk fast and good.

"Mother, oh please, just listen. I need a Toni. Everybody's getting one for the dance. I have baby-sitting money for it, but could you do it for me?" Mother purses her lips and squints her eyes—the thinking look. Might mean yes. "Today," I meekly add. Uh oh, she's slumping

113

one shoulder and raising her eyes to the ceiling. Might mean no.

"Well, Lily, why did you wait 'til now? How many times do I have to tell you I need warning for such stuff." I hang my head and shuffle a toe around on the floor, seems like five minutes. It works. "Well, all right," she gives in, "but we better put a move on."

"Lordy, that stuff stinks." Mother dabs the cold, drippy stuff on every little curler on my head, the hair wound so tight it takes my breath away. She leans over the box to see the directions laid out on the table. She jabs the number 4 step with her finger. "Okay, now, you have to sit awhile, then I'll pour the rinse on it. You set the timer on the stove for 10 minutes and call me when it dings." Nita already left the room a long time ago, holding her nose. Jack and Daddy had to go out to the garage to escape the kitchen turned into a beauty shop.

Guess I have time to call Pat right now to see what she's going to wear tomorrow night. She tells me hers and then I tell mine. "Yeah, sounds cute Patty. So, I have a baby pink sweater to go with my flared grey skirt. Probably need pearls too, huh? What shoes should I wear with …uh…Pat, better call you back. *Oh no*. I forgot to set the timer. "Mother, Mother, where are you? Hurry up!"

Sleeping on a wet head of hair isn't much fun, but it's way too late to stay up until it dries. Mother says we'll comb it out in the morning.

Can't *get* the comb out of it in the morning. It's stuck in the tumble weeds on my head. I could die, really, I want to die. The frizz is sticking out about a foot all over and the mirror is shouting to me, "looks like you're being electrocuted." I'm squeezing the mess and pressing it with my hands and wrapping a big wet towel around it. It's no use. I'm screaming and kicking the waste basket when Daddy bangs on the door. "Lily, what in the world is going on in there? Get out of that bathroom, right now. There are two of us waiting to get in there. Right now, hear me?"

Mother says there are three solutions. "Wear a hat, a cap or a scarf to the dance, cut off all the frizz or stay home. Stop blubbering and pick one."

"Cut it," I say," but who cuts it?"

"Not me," Mother shakes her head, "I don't want to take the blame for what it looks like. Nuh, uh."

My dialing finger gets numb from all those calls to the beauty shops. Nobody can squeeze me in. Mother sticks her head into the room. "I've got it Lily. Hear this. What is your father, Lily? Well, he is a barber, isn't he, Lily? A barber. He cuts hair!"

Well, she's gone crazy. My father cuts men's hair—in a man's barber shop. I see a cartoon bubble in my mind with me in my pink sweater, pearls and a crew cut. I'm hysterical. I'm horrified. I'm desperate.

I make Daddy pull all the blinds in his shop on Main street and hang out his sign that says "Out to lunch. Be back in 30 minutes." I can't believe I'm doing this. He can't believe he's doing this. Mother believes it and shoves the scissors in his hand. "Lester, get clipping. We don't have much time."

Daddy tries, but the electric clippers seem to have a mind of their own.

I make two dozen cookies to take to the dance for refreshments. I put on the fuzzy pink sweater and the skirt made for whirling around. I clasp the pearls around my neck and push my feet into the black patent leather wedgies. Wincing, I pull on Mother's pink cloche hat from last Easter, the brim resting on the top of my ears.

I go to the dance with Patty. She says pink is definitely my color. At least nobody laughs out loud when we come in, but I can see a little bunch of girls staring and whispering to each other. We sit on the bleachers in the gym watching to see who dances with who. Dennis, the new boy from my English class feels sorry for me, I guess, and asks me to jitter bug. I have to say no because I'm worried the pink hat might slip off. Nobody wants to slow dance with me. The bleacher seats get mighty hard after a while.

I come on home. I stomp on the Toni box. I cut it into a million pieces with Mother's cooking shears. I eat all of the 13 chocolate chip cookies left over from the dance, one hand holding up my sorry-mess head, it feeling like a stubble field of corn.

Hired Hand

Gosh. Boo Hall's house is the most beautiful thing I have ever seen. Daddy says Boo Hall's feed store on Main Street must be doing pretty danged good. This house is so big it covers almost half a block. It's white with green shutters opening up to windows that have square little panes, each one of them framed in polished wood. Velvety deep purple drapes, pulled back in loopy swags, show through the sparkly glass. Wide porches wind around the whole house. Next to the house is a garden without vegetables. Instead it has flowers and trees and white trellises with vines and blossoms dripping from them. And rolling down the little hill that the house rests on is a green lawn carpet, mowed every week by the hired hand.

I get to be a hired hand too. I can't wait.

Mrs. Boo Hall is going to pay me to watch Milton and Annie when she goes out someplace or when she gives a big dinner party. Today she opens the wide oak door when I knock, knock with the silver ring hanging out of a lion's mouth.

"Well, Lily, do come in and meet the children. You are just in time to put them down for a nap. But first, Milty needs a bath. He's such a dirt digger, that little rascal." She leads me into a living room bigger than a barn with fancy curlicued furniture and ornaments and cloth covered lamps on every table. Hanging down from the middle of the ceiling is a giant light all crowded around with twinkling little globs of glass. Gollee.

She puts on her big-brim white hat and white gloves to match and sticks a little beaded purse under her arm. "Good-bye dears," she croons with a pat on the head for each of them. "Lily will take good care of you while I'm at the tea party." The door closes soft-like behind her. Both of those little heads swivel around to look at me, big eyed. I smile at them, big-eyed.

"Well kids," I'm trying to put a friendly little giggle in my voice, "I guess it's about time for a nap. And a nice bath for Milton." I hold out both hands to them, one for each. Annie looks steely, stares at me, screams twice and falls like a wet dish rag on the floor. Milton bats away my hand, whoops, sounding like Indians crying war on the Lone Ranger. And then he hits his chest with his fists before racing down the middle of the room headed for the kitchen. By the time I catch up with him, bawling Annie slung on my hip, he's on top of a three-legged stool on his tippy-toes, stretched out toward what must be a cookie jar on top of the fridge.

My mistake, thinking back on it, was going for him when the stool started to tip, forgetting Annie, by now struggling and sliding down my leg. All of us are in a tangled-up heap down on the linoleum, sharp little spears of the cookie jar and chunks of peanut butter cookies scattered all over our bodies.

I'm real afraid of another Milty escape, so I search for leashes. Yeah. Mrs. Boo's big cooking apron is hanging on a cupboard knob. Victory! Tight tied to their Mother's apron strings, I lead them down the hall to the bedrooms and bath. I clutch them tight to me with one arm while I run water and pour in pink bubble bath for Milty. Thank the Lord— a big smile spreads all over his face, and he starts to strip off his clothes and climb into the tub, grabbing water toys off the wide rim as he sinks down into the bubbles.

I chance it. I leave Milton and take Annie into her bedroom. I stuff her under the blankets and throw books from the nightstand her way. I take a quick peek at Milty. Whew. He's busy with his boats and water pistol. I run back into Annie's room, trip over the books she slammed to the floor and slide feet first to the back wall of the room. I can hear her tee-hee-hee while I scramble up. What now? "Hey, Annie, want a story?"

Two picture books later she's sleeping, her hair sweat-plastered down on her forehead.

CRIPES! I FORGOT MILTON!! I crash down the hall to the bathroom. The boats and pistol float on the fizzed out bubbles. The floor is slippery with drips and small wet footprints. The room is silent.

The big oak door with the lion door knocker slams hard behind me. I race down the street, yelling, screaming, "Milty, Milton!" As I round the corner heading to Main Street, I see Milty's little pink bottom and very naked bony body heading for the Feed Store. I make it through the door, smelling the hay, just as Milty runs around the counter, jumps up and wraps his body around his Daddy's leg.

"Uh, Boo, no, Mr. Boo, uh Mr. Hall, sir. Milton…uh, sort of…got…away. I can hear my voice petering out and my heart booming. Mr. Boo stares me in the eyes.

Annie sleeps through it all. Milty gets sent to his room. Mr. Boo goes back to sell some more hay. Mrs. Boo pulls off her gloves, takes the pins out of her hat, pulls it off and sets it down on the sofa. She sighs. Two times.

"Lily, sit down," she says, motioning to the big leather chair. I'm waiting to be fired. She does.

122

But, you won't believe this. I get to go back to that beautiful house, to be another kind of hired hand—Mrs. Boo's right hand man ...uh...woman...girl. Oh, so much better. I get to be there for the big dinners, help her cook, serve the food (exactly how she shows me) and afterwards, almost scary, I wash and dry the gold decorated, see-through China dishes. Best of all I get to eat the left-over French onion soup and Steak Diane and the yummiest little quivery lemon tarts.

I do love tasting the life of rich folks.

Funerals

Dear Judy,

Do you like it in Los Angeles? Have you met James Dean yet? Do you have a new friend? I wish my oldest and best friend would come back. Really, I miss you so much. High school is okay, but if you were here it would be super. So, how about you go tell your folks I said that you can live here at my house and then just get on the bus and come!

But...it might be a little crowded, because my Granpa lives with us now. It's just for awhile though, because he gets passed around the family, like my cousin Henry did, but it was because Henry was a drunk, not because he was old.

Granpa goes to my Uncle Chester next. I guess when you're 87, you have to get taken care of and nobody wants the whole job. At least Nita and I get to keep our bedroom. Jack has to sleep on a pallet in the living room and scrunch all his clothes into a big box until Granpa goes or dies.

Granpa isn't much any fun anymore. He just sits in the rocker by the front window and stares out at the cars driving by. He has a chaw of tobacco in his mouth, like he always did, but it dribbles out of the side of his mouth and down his chin now. And he can't spit it out into an old can the way he used to. My mother puts a dish pan in his lap, so he can drool into that. He still tells stories, but in the middle of one he usually drops his chin down on his chest and snores. Good thing we already know the ends of them.

I wish we could pass him on to Uncle Chester right now. I have to clean up the mess after he eats and wash his underwear and help him shuffle around the house. Mother tells me everyday, "Now keep an eye on him, Lil. Don't let him wander off." And we can't bring friends over because it makes him jumpy and sometimes he pees, right there in his chair. I hope he doesn't die here while it's our turn.

Oh Jude! That makes me remember when we were in the 7th grade, and my Granma died and the relatives in Texas sent us a picture of her in the casket. She looked all pink and white and plump and satiny. That made us think up an adventure that summer, right? Remember that? We went around every other day or so to Kratzenheimer's Mortuary to check on funerals. We would sneak in, stepping over that one board we knew screeked, out in the hall. Then we poked our heads around the door to see if a casket was there on display. I don't remember how many bodies we saw, do you? How about old Mr. Bruner, huh? We could see his long pointy nose sticking up above the side of the

126

casket before we even peeked in! Giggles...oh man, we had to stuff our fists in out mouths, huh? Gardenias. That's what it smelled like in that cool room where the funeral was going to happen, and the music was floating all around us in there. We were lucky to get out, every time, before all the crying relatives came.

Well, Judy, guess I'd better end my letter, because it's time to feed Granpa, and I'll have to mop up after. I hate it. I know I shouldn't hate that he's here, but I do. I wish it was over!

I'll mail this as soon as I get a stamp. You write me, hear?

Love,

Lily

Dear Judy,

Thanks for your letter back. You sound happy in Los Angeles. I wish I could be there, instead of here.

I have bad news. It's over. Granpa is dead. I can't believe it. And I'm sick with feeling guilty. After I wrote you last time, Granpa threw up all over my new white bucks. I saved for three months to buy those shoes. I was so mad I screamed and stomped and told Daddy it wasn't fair to have Granpa so long at our house. Then I chased Daddy and followed him all over the house and outside for days whining about Granpa. Finally, he wrote to Uncle Chester, and we took Granpa over to his house in Modesto. We left him there, his watery, filmy eyes following us all the way out to the car.

The next week Uncle Chester called us in the middle of the night from the hospital. Granpa was dead. He and Aunt Wilma had to run to the store and while they were gone Granpa walked out the back door and fell off the porch. The doctor said he had a heart attack, but I know he died because there was no one there to watch him. I watched him at our house. If he hadn't left our house, he would still be alive. It's my fault, I just know it. I'm the one who bothered Daddy until he sent him away. I wished it. God is punishing me for wishing it.

I can't stand thinking about Kratenheimer's now. About the cool room and the gardenias. Now it's my crying relatives. I can't look in the casket. I just can't.

Please write back. I feel terrible.

Love, Lily

P.S. Hey, Jude. Do you think I could come live with you?

The Big Achieving Peace Speech

Mr. Darby tells me to practice in front of a mirror. "Use your voice and body to captivate the audience right away," he coaches. "This competition is keen; there will be very good speakers from all over the county. You'll have to project yourself extremely well."

I'm trying. I begin my speech to my dresser at home. "I am peace. Just a seedling now - spindly, frail and fragile, just beginning to grow..." A sickening feeling in my stomach stops me right in the middle of the sentence. That's not all Mr. Darby said when I practiced in front of him yesterday at school. "Well," he had cleared his throat, "your body doesn't exactly portray spindly or frail, I'm afraid. That could be a problem. Hmmmm." He stands back and scratches his little goatee. "Maybe it would help to wear something bucolic. You have anything like that?"

What the heck is bucolic?

"Oh sure, Mr. Darby," I nod.

The mirror over my dresser repeats what Mr. Darby said to me. I'm too round. No seedling here. Peace... fully developed... already. Two weeks left before the Bank of America speech contest. Can I do it? Well, maybe not spindly or frail, but at least some thinner. Starting today and every day I will eat no more than 500 calories, walk three miles and take long steam baths. And better look up bucolic.

"Lily, dammit. What are you doing in that bathroom so long? Get out of there, right now." Daddy yells and thumps on the door.

Dripping out of the tub, my pink body feels a little woozy. I don't think an hour is enough though. The scale doesn't think so either. Guess I'll have to do this at night after everybody goes to bed.

Okay then. It's carrots, lettuce and celery, Melba toast and gallons of water. Maybe just one tiny chocolate chip cookie.

And Jeez, what does a bucolic dress look like?

Mr. Darby drives me to the county seat for the first round of the contest, where everyone will be eliminated but two. He listens to me reciting in the car, prompts me, tells me to do my school proud and says my dress looks "sufficiently pastoral… agricultural - albeit somewhat Little Bo-Peepish."

Mr. Darby drives me home from the county seat.

He slaps the steering wheel. "By God, Lily, you did it! You absolutely did it!"

"Now, we have one week to really polish it," he says the next day. "That boy, Dexter, you're up against is very good—strong and convincing." Oh, great, I tell myself. I better get Mom to stock up on more lettuce.

Mr. Darby really believes I can win. We work on it everyday after school, and we are getting exited. I run and sweat and tell my growling stomach to shut up. Mother washes and carefully presses the bucolic dress we found at J.C. Penny's. It is pale green with puffy short sleeves, white buttons down the front, and lacey flounces around the neck and hem.

The Bank of America holds the banquet in a big, fancy hotel. There are many round tables with snowy white tablecloths and sparkly plates and glasses. Mr. Darby and I sit up at the front table with Dexter and his speech teacher, right next to the bank President and the judges. I can't eat. My bucolic dress shrunk with the washing and the buttons barely close. Nobody seems to notice. Dexter devours everything they serve.

After I give my speech, there is so much applause and Mr. Darby whispers in my ear after I sit down: "Flawless. Simply flawless." After Dexter finishes, there is so much applause that Mr. Darby whispers, "It will be very close."

The ice cream has melted in my dish, and the judges are still talking to each other. Dexter is finishing his second helping. Mr. Darby is twisting his napkin around his fingers but smiling a lot, too.

After about a year, there is a tap, tap, tapping on the microphone. Every spoon shushes. Every head raises. The head judge stands up and looks over the audience. He moves the microphone up a bit to reach his mouth. "It was a very difficult decision, since both speakers were excellent. But, we are ready to announce the winner."

My fingers tremble in my lap, my empty stomach flutters, my heart thunders under my bucolic buttons. My ears await my name.

The judge declares: "Dexter Drummond, please come up to the stage. Congratulations!"

Mr. Darby pats my shoulder, says I did a great job, says it was just so close, you know, nothing to feel bad about. On the way home though, he slumps behind the wheel, his tie hanging loose down his shirt and his face sagging, to match. He drops me off at home where the front porch light seems too bright. I quietly open the front door, glad that Mother and Daddy are asleep. I can't bear to look at their faces when I tell them. I am sick at the sight of the huge plate of chocolate chip cookies Mother has left out on the dining room table for me. I'm shocked that I didn't win. I just know Dexter Drummond didn't have to work as hard as I did—the big jerk.

I run out of the house. I finally cry...in the dark...on the grass...up on the big hill two streets from our house. It hurts...more than anything ever did before. I failed. I wasn't good enough.

What? All of a sudden, Jeez, Daddy's face is here, looking right into mine, a flashlight dangling from his hand. "Lily, dammit, we've been looking all over for you. Come on home, now."

He steers me by my elbow down the hill and into the house. Mother is making hot chocolate in her night gown and smiling that special "I'm sorry, Lily." Daddy tells me he's proud anyway—so proud, dag nabbit, that I can stay in the bathroom as long as I want—for a whole week.

Boys

November 5, 1949

Dear Diary,

This is awful. I thought Eddie really liked me. But now he never even looks at me. I want to die. And he's sooo cute. What happened? Now, there's no one. All I ever do is hang around with Jen and Marie and Betty...the smart girls, good girls. Boring girls. Ugh.

Life is terrible.

December 11, 1949

Well, Diary, I have a new friend. Her name is Elena. She's Spanish. Not Mexican, she makes sure I know that. And get this, she has two big brothers and her brothers know all the guys! Every night we call each other to plan what we will wear the next day. We even made twin jumper dresses (Mother helped us) to wear to the next dance. She's so much fun...silly, wiry and full of energy, black eyes flashing. Mother says (with that little frown on her brow) that she's high spirited. One of the best parts of being Elena's friend is that boys come over to their house all the time!

January 15, 1950

Dearest Diary,

I have to remember to lock you up today after I write. Because, I will tell you about the big party I went to last night. We all met – lots of kids, at Elena's house. We joked and fooled around for awhile and then we all drove out to the hills in back of town. It was raining some, but not too much at first. Helen's brothers brought beer and everybody sat in the mud and drank it. Except I really didn't—because you're not supposed to until you're 21, you know. I just pretended and poured out my can when no one was looking. Most of the kids were really drunk and slid down the hill in the pouring rain, shoving each other around all crazy like. On the way home Elena necked in the back seat with her new boyfriend Joe, and I sat in front worrying about Harry Wilson crashing the car, every time he tried to grab my leg. Good thing I spent the night at Elena's. Don't tell, Diary. Mother and Daddy would kill me.

February 12, 1950

Wow, Diary,

Guess what? I'm going to have a date with Danny Walton! I can't believe it. He's home from college and asked me to go to a movie. Me! What would he see in me? He's such a doll and dresses sharp and has his own car. I can't wait to tell Elena. We have to figure out what I'll wear and whether to do a pony-tail or not.

February 15, 1950

Diary,

It was horrible. We watched the movie at the drive-in—sort of. Danny kept wanting to neck all the time. He didn't even get us any popcorn or soda at the snack shack. And after, he drove us out to the spot on the hill where everybody goes to make out. Well, one thing led to another and I was trying hard not to do anything, but not make him mad either. I hate it. What do you do? I said I had to go home. So, he let go of my boobs, which he had been mooshing, it seemed like forever. He turned on the engine in a hurry and didn't even walk me to the door when we got home.

March 19, 1950

Dear Diary,

This is awful. Danny never called again. Here's the worst of it. Elena says her big brothers overheard Danny at the gas station talking to his college buddies. He was bragging on how he went out with me on a dare, because I had the biggest boobs in town.

I am sick to death. I'm through with boys, Diary, I swear!

Work

"You see, Lily, it's like this: Wish in one hand and ..." I stop him with *my* hand. "I know, I know. No need to tell me again about wishing and spitting." It's sure not the first time Daddy spouted this one to me, but now I really get it. It goes right along with "Work never hurt aaanybody." That means stop asking about a new bathing suit and find a way to get the money for it yourself.

Well, it's not like I don't try. But that green and yellow plaid, stretchy suit with the little bitty straps costs way more than I can make baby sitting. Last month when I was desperate for a new pair of jeans, I even waited tables at Pete's café, down there across from Boo Hall's feed store. It was a disaster, I'm telling you. Taking the orders was bad enough and trying to clip the order slip on that shiny metal wheel whirling around was a mess. The worst was bringing the grilled cheese to Mrs. Kraus, when she wanted tomato soup and then serving old man Brewster sunny-side up instead of over-easy. They could show a little patience, I thought. Pete thought different, and I got fired after two days. Just as well. Mr. Kaufman, the beer delivery man, kept trying to pinch my bottom when I leaned over to clean up the milk shake that spewed out all over the room. Well, I tried to tell Pete anybody could forget to push that little button that says "lock" on the side of the blender.

So, now what? Somebody's going to snap up that little suit if I don't hurry up and spit.
While we're doing the dishes, I try to soften up Mother. "I promise I'll do all the housecleaning and all the ironing for a month, if you'll just loan me the money." Well, she doesn't even answer me—like she never heard a word of it!

But, she does turn around from her stove burner scrubbing and mention a new job up at the Country Club. "They're wanting high school girls to spend the weekends working in the outdoor restaurant."

" Oh Mother," I groan. "You know I'm a terrible waitress…and I hate it."

"Just shush now and listen. You don't have to take orders or serve people. It's a buffet and all you do is set up the tables and carry out the food and arrange and keep the dishes full. That's a snap, right?"

They pick us up on the corner of Main Street by the feed store and drive us out to the Country Club in a big, long station wagon. First, they show us the room all four of us will stay in for the weekend and hand out starchy pink and white uniforms and ugly black hair nets. Then we line up in front of the manager out on the patio. Now, picture this: a tall man, dressed up in his Sunday-go-to-meetin' clothes. He has a gray shiny suit with a bright, white, stiff as a board shirt and a blue striped tie. Eyes traveling on down his legs, you can see peeking out from the pressed pants cuffs the most spotless light grey suede shoes I have ever seen. His blond hair is all swept up in a pompadour and not one single whisker hair can be seen on his face. He walks around us, making sure we are presentable, and now and then flicks at his pants or shoes to make sure no dust or dirt clings on. A mighty sharp dresser, that's what Daddy would call him. I call him a big "stuck-on-himself."

He's in charge, though, and I'd better call him by his name. It's a funny name, and I keep having to ask Elena to remind me what it is and finally she whispers, "Jeez Lily, it's Pimber, just remember rhymes with timber, okay? And don't ask me again."

Well, the work is not exactly what I would call a snap. We have to fill all the dishes with the buffet food and carry them out to the long, white clothed tables, being sooo careful not to spill a drop or a crumb. The Dandy Dresser stands around, making sure we do it fast, sort of clucking and shaking his head when one of us makes a mistake. It's an Italian dinner, and I am in charge of the spaghetti with steamy tomato sauce that is served from huge white platters. Mr. What's-His-Name tilts his head and cocks his eye at me if I let the platter get empty, so on this trip to the kitchen I fill it to the brim. I'm hurrying around the corner to get out of the kitchen, eyes glued to the slopping red sauce, when BAM! I run into a body coming into the kitchen.

It looks like blood, real red blood with white strings, laid generously upon a… light grey suede shoe. Setting the platter on the floor, I swipe furiously at the shoe with my pink apron, apologizing with feeling. "Oh, Mr. Plumber (I hesitate briefly…yeah, right… like lumber), Mr. Plumber I am so sorry!"

Please, God, let lightening strike me right now because I'm already a goner. Mr. Plumber (or whatever his name is…I'm not so sure now) screams at me. "Get away from me, you idiot! Get out of here, right now!"

I get out all right, but I look over my shoulder as I am running up to the room. Well, it is a pretty sorry sight. That man, that picky, picky Mr. Whatever is sitting on a chair on the buffet patio, holding his waved up head in his manicured hands… simpering and whimpering. Up in the room I strip off the pink and white uniform and ugly black hairnet, whip on my jeans and shirt and head out the door for home.

Six miles is a lot longer than you'd think. But there is a lot of time to sort things out too. It doesn't even take a half a mile, though, to realize I am not going to get that bathing suit. And for sure I was never meant to be a waitress or even a snap buffet server. I wish Daddy had an old Texas saying for this situation.

Tonight after I tell the whole pitiful story, Daddy leans back real slow in his kitchen chair and gives it to me, somber like: "Lily," his voice is down real deep, " just don't cry over spilt..." then his eyes squint up into a crinkly smile and he slaps his leg "...spaghetti sauce."

Fashion

Not a sock in the house. Well, anyway, not the kind I need. Searching every corner of my dresser drawers again isn't going to help. And even the dirty clothes hamper is empty, the washing machine chugging away. Dang! And it's almost time to leave for school. No white socks to wear with my white bucks! But I have to have white. It is an absolute MUST. Nobody would be caught dead wearing any other color with white bucks. So, think fast. Okay, who else has socks? Mother doesn't wear socks. Daddy's are black and brown and ribby and shiny...ugh. Nita's socks are doll size. Jack....hmmm. Let's go look.

Oh man, I'm out of luck. Jack doesn't have any either. This is desperate. What to do now? Well...the next best (but not good at all) would be to try to match my outfit. Trying to stay calm, I look at my skirt which is kind of brown and black plaid with a little dark red. Would Jack have anything to go with that? What a jumbled mess, socks snaked around in every drawer, not one pair tucked inside each other like Mother showed us to do. Boys. Wait...here's one. It could work. It's the right size and matches my skirt. Now is there another one in this rat's nest? Yes! Here it is.

I pull them on as fast as I can. Oh drat, one has a hole in the heel. I kind of roll and pull the top of the sock over the hole and make the other sock look the same. It looks really dumb, but no time left.

I practice walking to school with my heels flat so as not to let the hole creep out. I look so stupid. Nobody ever wears socks like this. Everybody will laugh and titter behind my back. It's bad enough that there are only three shoe string holes in my white bucks, instead of four, like the ones everyone else wears. Mother says we have to get these because they are at least $5.00 cheaper than the Spauldings. I just know this is part of the reason I'm not real popular, like the stuck-up cheerleader girls. They all know what to wear, all the time—and do. Who starts it all, anyway? I don't get it. Who started all of us wearing what's IN?

Well, if I had to guess, it would be the girl I see right now coming up to the big front doors of our school the same time as me. Ramona Howard, that's who, the most glamorous, popular girl of all. Lord, I can't believe it; she's staring right at me—surveying every detail top to bottom. Maybe if I open the door for her and swing it wide back to cover me, she won't spy the horrible socks.

"Hi, Lily!" The door trick doesn't work. Ramona's eyes are locked on my feet. "Lily, what cuuute socks! I like the way you turned them down like that...really cool. Where did you buy them?"

Now what? My brain is spinning around in my head, trying to find a lie that would work. "Uh, well. Well...yeah." Suddenly, the words come out of somewhere. "My cousin, she lives in Dallas, she sent them to me. They're really IN in Dallas, you know."

Ramona cocks her cute little head sideways a bit. "Huh. Well, see you later," she trills, striding into the hallway, blond pony-tail swishing elegantly behind her, bouncy foot steps in her perfect white socks and pristine white bucks. Spauldings, of course.

I shuffle in, taking my time, hoping she'll spread the good word before I run into any one else. I whisper a little to myself. "Thank you Lord. This was close. I owe you one."

The Big Block A

These are the worst feelings I know: one, the last to be picked in a neighborhood baseball game (even four-eyes-Chuck isn't last); two, not catching the fly ball when the game depends on it; three, looking stupid when you strike out every time; four, not making the team—any team.

Texans love sports. Maybe that's why I love sports. Crave sports. Eat, sleep, live for sports. Today, Daddy's little radio blares out the game from the Oakland Oaks stadium where they duel with their arch rival, the San Francisco Seals. Jack and I stretch out on the living room floor, ears close to the speaker, our fingers aching from crossing them so long. We're praying for an Oaks miracle in the ninth inning. Holding your breath is so delicious, so excruciating.

But, listening and watching and screaming until your voice quits and knowing all the stats for all the teams and wearing the colors and the cap...is not playing. I want to play.

In the spring, Elena and I try out for the baseball team. Miss Gottlieb is one tough, mean, ex-marine gym teacher, and we know we are in for brutal practices if we make the team. I don't care. Elena cares. Elena hates sweat. It's hard enough to convince her to do it with me. I hope she won't back out when we start gasping and dripping salty perspiration out on the field.

"Get your butts movin'!" Miss G screams a lot. "Throw that ball overhand—we don't tolerate any girlie throws," she growls at me. "Good God, Lily, can't you hit anything? Come on, scrunch down, knees and feet together. Don't let that ball go through your legs again, do you hear me?" It's not looking good for me.

"All right women, muster up." Clip board propped on her raised bare knee, Gottlieb balances like a stork out there in the dusty field. She barks out the names of the girls who make the team. "The rest of you can go home," she commands, immediately turning her back on the losers and hustling up the winners to start the practice. I go home. Elena stays.

You know what, though, it turns out maybe old Gottlieb has a heart, after all. The next day she calls me into her office in the gym. "Lily, you're a lousy baseball player. Actually you're pretty lousy at most sports. But… you know…you can run. Fast. And long. I'm trying to get together a field hockey team. How about it...you in?"

Oh man, if she only knew. I'd say "sure" to tiddely-winks or even goldfish gulping.

"Uh, what's field hockey, Miss G?"

Yep, you do run in field hockey. And yep, I'm good at it. It's the little hard ball and the hockey stick part that gets me. Miss Gottlieb says I'd better shape up or ship out. I'm not shipping out. Every single day, after school until dark and Saturday and Sunday too, I run like a ninny with that stick and ball—pushing it, rolling it, whacking it, passing it to an imaginary teammate, struggling to drive the blasted thing into the goal.

It's a banner day, all right, when I make the team and get the purple and gold uniform with the silly belt that makes you look lumpy below the waist. I have to say our team is a pretty sorry looking bunch of girls, and we're so bad Gottlieb has to schedule games as far away as Manteca because schools around here don't want us losers. Okay with me...I'm playing!

The school bus leaves at 5:00 o'clock in the morning for the Manteca game, and I can't stop my legs from shivering in my purple shorts or my bottom from bouncing on the cold metal seat. I don't even know where Manteca is, but I can smell it waaay before we get there. It's real country out here, for sure. Seems like cows own the place. There's a big open grassy-weedy field behind the school where we play, and it's still so early the grass is drippy wet.

The Manteca girls are big and beefy, ready to demolish us. And they do, but so far (a miracle) there is no score: the game is 0 to 0. All of a sudden, close to the end of the game, I get the ball, passed to me in mid-field. My heart hammers. I clutch the stick and move the ball, whap, whap, this way, that way—fast—down the field. I can hear feet, pounding behind me, a moose of a Manteca girl close on my heels, her stick stretching out to scoop away the ball. She's got it!

"CRAP!!" I shout. Really…crap. The mammoth Manteca girl slithers and slides through a mushy mound of Manteca cow poop. And, holy cow, she loses the ball! I slash it away and head, hell bent and legs pumping, straight to the goal. I give the ball a mighty whack and I score. WE WIN 1 – 0!!

Oh, the glory of it. Sure, there's no one to cheer except our team and Miss G. No cheerleaders, no fans, no band. No matter. I played and I scored and we won our first ever game.

And, oh yes, let me tell you about the sweetest moment of all. The scene is the end of the year sports award ceremony. All of the school is there in the auditorium. Parents are there. The band and the cheerleaders are there. I am there. Miss Gottlieb, a little crooked grin on her face, hands me the coveted, official, BIG BLOCK A, purple with glowing gold trim. It tells the world:

152

I am an athlete. I will sew it on my purple school sweater and wear it to every game of every sport every year of high school. And I will keep it forever, in my cedar chest, wrapped carefully in crispy tissue with a moth ball on top.

Being One of Them

Mother starts in again, between bites of her mayonaisey tuna fish sandwich. Starts on who it is she wishes I would be more like.

"Astrid Norenberger!" I try not to scream it too loud, but honestly, you know, this is sickening. Reeeaally, of all the drippy girls in the whole, entire high school, she wants me to be like Assstrid! "Mother, just her name! Can't you picture the kids snorting behind their hands when the teacher calls her name at roll call?"

Mother grabs up a paper napkin and expertly stops the drool of sandwich goo heading down her chin. "Well, Lily, she can't help her name. I'm talking about how polite she is, how she never makes a grade lower than A plus, how she dresses...well, how sweet and mindful of her parents and how she has nice friends."

Now, I get it. Mother is not liking that I got invited to a party where there will be "fast" kids. Fast, for her, does not mean athletic. It means doing things that nice girls wouldn't do. I guess that means nice girls would be slow. Anyway, I tell her that this party is with girls only, a slumber party. So, there's no chance to be fast.

Well, I am definitely dying with excitement. Cherise actually invited me to her

155

house to spend the night with popular girls! Trudy and Monica and Susan...all close to the top of the heap! I can't figure it out. Cherise has always snubbed me, tittered behind my back, called me teacher's pet and turned her head when I walk by her in the hall. I don't really like her, but she has all the right friends. I don't know and don't care why she changed her opinion of me, and I can't wait to go.

I don't even know what popular girls sleep in. Do they put rollers in their hair at night? What kind of toothpaste do they use? Do they stay awake all night and gorge on potato chips and coke and chocolate chip cookies—like unpopular girls do? I have to think about all this, so I can do it right. Who knows where this might lead if I can pull it off. Me, popular. Gee whiz.

Friday night, Mother drives me to the party that's going to start at 7:00 o'clock. Cherise's house is a really big one way up on a grassy hill just outside of town, where bright mustard weeds and golden poppies are poking up their colors. As we drive up the windy road, Mother tells me she loves those California poppies, but wishes there were some Texas Bluebonnets, too. "Guess they just don't transplant as well as we do," she mumbles to herself.

Cherise has made a map so we can find the way. We allowed a lot of time to get here, so it's a little early when we pull up into the driveway by their front entrance door. We both gawk. It is almost the size of the whole front of our house. The red brick house is two stories high, with sparkling windows all around, outlined by gleaming white shutters. I think you might call it a mansion.

Last night, Mother let me use her blue Samsonite overnight case to put my stuff in. I packed two sets of P.Js. One pink and frilly and one jazzy, crazy orange. I can decide which one when I see what the others wear. I brought two kinds of toothpaste, for the same reason. Rollers, just in case, along with a brand new blue brush— not one snarled hair anywhere in the spiky bristles. I stuffed in a top and another pair of blue jeans for tomorrow morning.

Oh gosh. I feel so nervous. I want to wait some in the car to see who shows up first and then I can go in with them. Not good to be first, because I may not know what to do, how to act. We wait. Then we wait some more. The sun goes down. I strain my ears trying to hear tires coming up the driveway. It's 7:30. It's dark. We are the only ones here.

"Lily, you better go ring the door bell. See if anyone is home."

I do. And no one is. I do again and
again. And no one comes.

It's 8:00. Mother says "Let's go home." I
say,"Let's wait just a little longer."

My stomach makes a flip-flop. This can't
be. Did I get it wrong? Maybe it's tomorrow
night. I finally nod that we can go home. There
is no slumber party with popular girls tonight.
get home I call on the phone to Cherise's house.
Of course no one answers. I have to look in the
phone book to find Trudy's number. Her mother
says she is with Cherise at Monica's house. After
the phone rings four times at Monica's, someone
picks it up. What I hear are girls giggling and then
some shushing. "Hello Monica? This is Lily. Is
Cherise there?"

"Yep, we're all here," she whoops. "But
you're not, dummy." Everyone is screaming and
laughing and shouting into my ear, "April Fool!"
Click.

It's a long time before I stop shaking and
crying and pulling things out of the overnight bag,
throwing them up against the wall, kicking them,
beating them with my fists.

Mother won't let me stay home from school on
Monday morning.   After first period everyone is
rooting around in their lockers, crashing the doors
closed, yelling at each other. Behind Cherise's

locker door, a little bunch of girls are whispering and laughing, shifting their eyes my way when they think I'm not looking.

I stand tall and hold up my head and mosey down the hall. Maybe I can catch up with Astrid Norenberger.

Snow Day

"Lily, listen to this!" You won't believe it, honest." It's Elena, babbling, spewing out her words so fast I can almost feel the spit coming through the ear piece of the phone. But then, Elena's always excited. Spanish blood, her mother explained one time.

"Hey, Elena, could you slow down a minute. What about snow?" We're supposed to be talking about what to wear to school today but it sounds like she's lost her marbles instead.

"Mt. Diablo...there's snow on it, Lil! Really, lots of it! The radio says so. And get this. A bunch of kids are going to ditch school and go up to play in it. Barb and Pam and Frankie and Ed and Marie...and me, I'm going. What do you think, you too?"

I'm thinking she's nuts. I, the owner of a gilded, official certificate, propped up on my dresser, declaring that I had perfect attendance, every single day, clear through all eight years of grade school. And so far, my record holds in high school too. I can't imagine skipping school even for snow—a weather condition so rare around here that there will be big, fat headlines in the newspaper.

No way. I mean, not a chance. I never missed a day of school all that time because Mother and Daddy made me go—no excuses, sick or not. Unless you needed to see Doc Shanks, you weren't sick enough. And I wasn't about to go to ol' shot needle Shanks. So, just ditching? They'd kill me. Truly, dead at fifteen.

But snow? My brain keeps on letting pictures of it creep in. Really? Gosh darn. I've never seen it. Never touched it, tasted it, rolled in it, slid on it. Maybe I'll never see it. Miserable, grabbing up my books, the idea creeps up on me, and I can't stomp it down. Shoot. What's the worst that can happen? I'm dying here, anyway, wanting to go so bad.

"El, is it too late? To go with you guys—to the snow?" Her shriek blasts through the phone line. "Yay! Not too late, but hurry. Pick you up in twenty minutes. Bye." It's perfect, meant to be, I think. Everybody—already gone from the house. Nobody to stop me. What to wear though?

Well, it shouldn't have been jeans, it turns out. Man, cold and wet, tight jeans are brutal. But the snow is crazy wonderful, beautiful, sparkling in the sun and deep enough to slide down on old inner tubes that Ed rounded up from his father's shop. We slap each other in the face with snow balls, roll around down the hills, until we look like ice-crusted monsters. Then we pull ourselves up the hill again, grabbing onto twiggy, leafless shrubs to hoist ourselves higher and higher. Fun, fun, fun…tingly, breathing hard, laughing until you almost pee in your pants fun!

Speaking of pee, wonder how you do that out here? Finally, the girls all find scraggly bushes to squat behind, and the boys use their handy tools to stream out their initials in the snow. At least that's what they brag about later when we come on down the mountain.

Well, like Mother says, "God works in mysterious ways." And Daddy brings up another ol' Eddards saying to fit the occasion: "Don't chew on anything you can't swallow." Turns out the worst punishment for ditching school isn't getting killed by your parents. It's having to go to Doc Shanks because you itch so bad you could scream, because you've got fiery, oozing, crusty, scaly rashy little bumps all over your body. I mean aaall over. And you've got fat blisters between your fingers, so big you can't use your hands. And you leak out icky, sticky, gluey fluid, seeping into the sheets so bad that Mother has to change them over and over every night. Your face is so swollen you look like the Pillsbury Doughboy. You are blind when you wake up in the morning—eye lashes stuck to your face. All of this bad, really bad stuff spells out POISON OAK in five foot letters.

Dr. Shanks can hardly find a bare spot to stick that needle in, but of course he finally does. "Put her in a cold tub of water with a lot of baking soda in it and leave her there a long time. Wrap those dripping arms and legs with clean rags, and you can use some Clorox to sponge on the worst itching places. Bring her back if she's not better in a few days."

I wasn't, so she did. I get shot again, and the Doc tells Mother to go to the ice house and get lots of chipped ice and pack me in it in the bathtub. Lying there, numb in that freezing ice, I murmur, looking heavenward, "Dear Lord, how long do I have to pay for my sins?"

Longer, God must have decided. Because, after all the itching stops and the oozing quits and my face shrinks to normal, I still look like a mottled monster. One more trip to Doc Shanks. "Might have scars," he says.

"Forever?" I gasp.

"Maybe... some," he says, almost kindly. He tells Mother, "Go get some Olive Oil and have her slather it all over when she's outside in the sun. Might help, might just take care of most of it."

I know one thing for sure. No chance of a golden "perfect attendance" certificate for high school. I guess I know one other thing for sure, too. You don't need to touch "leaves of three" to get poison oak. Bare winter branches will do the job. Yes siree.

My Party

Elena's leaping body sends the fishing poles and probably a million plastic bags of fiching hooks and flies sailing across the garage.

"CRIMINENTLY!" Her screaming sends the spider scuttling, real quick, to another dark corner. I stick my pointer fingers in my ears. "I'm getting out of here Lily. I HATE spiders." She heads for the door.

"Come on, El, I'll get the bug spray, okay?"

"Not okay," the sparks in her black eyes say, while she grabs up her jacket. "Call me when it's clean and I'll help you with the cokes and stuff."

Great. What a webby, dusty, oily, gasoline-smelly old place this is, and I have to clean it up by myself, and it's got to be fast. Maybe I could pay Jack or Nita to help me. Naaahh. I have to use that money to pay back Mother for the new jeans I'm going to wear tonight. "Oh, poop, just get at it," I tell myself out loud.

I sort of can't wait, but I sort of don't want it to come, either. I never gave a party before. What if nobody comes—well, except Elena, Pat and Marie. They promised, no matter what. But, Geez, hope some boys come. How stupid if no boys come. Probably Leroy and Harold though. But the popular guys—will they? We didn't invite any popular girls.

Well, it's good enough in here. All the junk is shoved back along the wall, the bug spray smell is almost gone, the cracked concrete floor is swept up and some benches and lawn chairs are spread around. The old rusty refrigerator has the cokes getting cold, and the record player is all plugged in. Just the potato chips and we're set.

It's just before eight and I'm spreading on my lipstick when Daddy comes in to give me the lecture. "No beer, no neckin', no loud music, and I'll be checking up every once in a while, hear?"

"Yep, for sure, Daddy." Boy, am I nervous. I put up a sign in the front yard saying PARTY OUT IN THE GARAGE. Don't want the door bell to keep bothering Mother and Daddy. Can't be too careful.

Elena and I jitter-bug around the record player while we wait … and wait, not saying to each other what we're worried about. Okaay! Finally, here come the first ones–both girls we expected. And… whew! I let out a breath because I hear a couple of cars pulling up in the driveway. Next thing you know, the garage is full of kids. Wow, I can't believe it. Even some of the football team come. There's Freddie (he is sooo adorable) and Larry (he's really nice and funny and smart) and Carl (he's so stuck up, I'm amazed he's here.) And, yay, everybody's dancing and joking and laughing. It's so much fun I forget to fill up the potato chip bowl again and don't even notice Daddy until he comes up to me.

"Lily, come outside in the front yard. I have to talk to you." When we get outside under the porch light, I can see he has that sharp, stony-bony, mean-eyed look—like when I come home too late or don't do the dinner dishes when I'm supposed to.

"Oh," I rush to make it right. "I'll turn the music down right now Daddy."

"No, Lily, that's not it. Get that Larry guy out." His voice is low and gravely and hateful. I don't get it, what does he mean?

"What are you talking about?"

"You know what. Just tell him to go."

"Why, Daddy? Nobody's drinking beer or necking. Especially not Larry, he's the nicest guy on the football team."

"Lily," he grabs hold of my arm and spits the words in my ear. "He's a nigger. I won't have a nigger on my property, do you hear me!"

I hear. I'm beginning to shake from the inside out. My knees feel so weak. My heart is going thud, thud, thud in my ears. I wonder if this is what fainting is. I lose my voice. My tongue is stuck. I will it to move, to shape the words I finally scream at him: "This is not right, Daddy! You are so wrong, wrong. Why do you hate like this? What did Larry ever to do to you? I like, like, really like Larry! Don't you trust my judgement? Would I like someone who is bad? What does a color have anything to do with a person? I hate you! I can't do it. I won't do it!"

Daddy grabs me by the shoulders and shakes me hard. "You tell him or I will, and I don't think you want me to!"

I feel so sick and I don't know what to do. I finally whisper, tears filling up my eyes. "Okay, I'll do it. In just a minute." I run into the house, past Mother who is twisting a dish towel between her fingers with her back turned to me, staring out the kitchen window. In the bathroom, I sit on the toilet lid, trying to get up my courage. How can I do this? Maybe tell everybody that my father says we are too loud and the neighbors are complaining and the party has to break up. Maybe tell them I just got sick; I have the flu and I'm contagious, so they all better go home. Maybe…what? What will they believe if I make something up? How can I not hurt Larry? It *will* hurt, no matter what. Oh Lord, what to do?

Daddy kicks at the bottom of the bathroom door. "Get out there, Lily. This is your last warning." Like a robot, I go out and whisper to Larry that I would like to talk to him out in front. He ambles over and leans against our flaky white painted fence, crosses his arms over the front of his letter jacket and stretches his long legs out in front of him. He's smiling his warm, wonderful way at me. When I finish telling him what my father wants, he closes up his smile, straightens up from the fence and asks me to tell his buddies he had to go home. I can't stop the hot, gushing tears. I run after him, taking his big hands in mine. "Oh Larry, I am so sorry. It hurts so much to do this. I hate it. I hate my father. I hate it all."

He drops his hands from mine, looks down at his scrubbed bright white tennis shoes and softly murmurs, "I know, I know. I'll go." I watch him take long strides down the driveway, his hands jammed in his pockets, and his head dropped toward his chest.

A long-time-ago memory blazes suddenly in my brain. It's that night back in the little Texas shack, when they don't know I hear them talking. Mother and Daddy, you were right!

I don't fit in this family—the whole family, uncles, aunts, cousins, brother, sister. I'm different.

I don't believe what you believe. I don't think the way you think. I can't be what you are. I'll never be one of you.

I don't get to fight back this time though. Larry and his family move away from our town—the summer of my party

The Try Outs

Rah, rah, rah, siss, boom, bah!
Amador Dons, rah, rah, rah!

"Girls, girls," Daddy yells from the kitchen. "Ya'll have mercy on the house, tone it down, hear?"

"Take a break," I say.

We throw the pom-poms in a corner and flop our bodies onto the carpet. Pretty sorry looking lot—breathing heavy, sweat glossy on our faces. The thing is, first off, we're mismatched: short, tall, skinny, fat and in-between. I'm the in-between, pretty much medium everything, boring, real blah. Elena calls Mary and Maureen, Mutt and Jeff, Mary being five-eleven and Mo topping out at five. Elena is her usual bony-skinny-minny self and Babs is ...well...what Texans call fleshy or heavy set. Daddy says it's a lot of beef on the hoof (Texans can be mean). The five of us together, jumping around the living room? We look more like a comedy act than a cheerleading team.

But, second of all, nobody but Babs can do the routine. Got every move just right, perfect, with the little jello jiggles of her stomach and thighs and her bountiful behind. Boom, boom. Right with the beat. She is *good*. We need her.

When the panting eases up, mild little Mo gets brave. "Lily, this is stupid. Who's going to vote for us? Not even the rest of the misfits will. You know they'll go with the crowd, trying to be part of it. And the crowd loves the popular girls—Cherise, Ramona, Monica. They're going to win, you know it."

"Yeah," Elena pipes up. "This is a mess. We can't even begin to look good...except for Babs. Let's give it up." Too tall Mary nods and nods, stretching out her pelican legs under the coffee table. Babs picks lint out of her belly button hanging over the snapped elastic of her shorts.

I stare them down. "We WILL do it." I spit it out like a drill sergeant. I told you we have to provide the competition...it's the American way (Poly Sci, this semester). We can't just let them win without a fight. Wimps, we can't be wimps. We represent the underdogs of the world. We'll set the example for...for...courage and conviction. Isn't this the land of equal opportunity? (American History, last semester). Get up women, be strong. Babs, lead us off!"

Today is it. The tryouts. We wear the colors: our purple gym shorts and T-shirts, snitched from our brothers and boiled into bright yellow in a smelly pot of dye on the stove, last night at home. Except for Babs. At the last minute her Dad wouldn't let her dye his only white double-extra-large he loaned her for the day.

We're first up, nervous, real nervous waiting in the wings of the stage. The all blond, all thin, all coordinated populars wait behind us. The whole student body is restless out there in the auditorium, wanting action. We hear our cue, Mr. Frasier announcing: "And now our cheerleading competition will begin." He motions to us with his bony finger.

It's not too bad. We jump and twirl, almost together. We slash our pom-poms left and right, up and down, only dropping one. We march and yell. We shout, "Gimme an A, gimme an M; gimme an A, gimme a D, gimme an O, an R - Amador! Yay, Yay, Yay."

And now the finale. We line up like can-can girls, kicking high. We're going to peel off, each one, doing a little hustle your bottom dance as we each leave the stage. Babs is the leader, of course. Here she goes, turning her back, smiling big and toothy over her shoulder. She bends over a little, bottom in the air, a perfect shimmy to the beat. Rah, Rah, Siss, boom...brrrr-aaaat! Babs lets go with the biggest poot in the world. Mother says I have to call it a poot. The boys call it an f-a-r-t.

Silence. A tomb of total silence in the room. Then the boys begin to stand up and clap and stamp their feet and whistle with their fingers between their teeth. The girls giggle behind their hands and jab elbows into their neighbor's ribs. Babs runs off the stage, her hands covering her face. I make the other girls finish the routine. "We are not quitters," I hiss.

It takes a month and nineteen chocolate sundaes to bring Babs back. We all chip in.

Rah. Rah. Rah. Siss boom bah.

Going Steady

I just don't know. I really haven't thought about it before, but maybe it's time. Especially since Elena is all ga-ga about Joe and spends all of her time with him. I can't believe she's actually thinking about getting married right after we graduate! Cripes, how scary that is.

So, how will I decide? Maybe I'll make two lists: one for all of the good reasons and one for all of the bad reasons. I'll title the page with "Should I get a steady boy friend?" and then I'll head each list with "Yes" or "No".

The Yes list:
1.   I would have someone to go to all of the dances with.
2.   I would look cool in his letter sweater, wearing his class ring.
3.   I would probably get invited to more parties.
4.   I could show him off to my cousins.
5.   I wouldn't have to worry about saying no anymore to the creepy guys who ask for dates.

The No list:
1.   I might feel tied down.
2.   I might get bored with just one guy.

3.   I might find somebody better.
4.   I would feel bad breaking it off.
5.   I would die if he broke up with me!

Oh shoot! It's a tie. Well, maybe I'll just keep my eyes open to see if there is anyone I could really like…enough.

We get paired up in Spanish class. "Como se llama?" he says. I try not to laugh. It's the worst accent I have ever heard. But I do notice what cool eyes he has when he cracks up at his own words.

"Me llama es Lilita" (it's what Mrs. Vardon says my name would be in Spanish). "Y usted?" I ask back.

"Juan." He giggles. "Really, John," he whispers, kind of close to my ear. Mmm, smells good. Old Spice, I think.

Whack! Mrs. Vardon taps his head with her ruler. "No ingles, si?"

She swishes off grandly to hover over another pair of struggling Spanish learners, allowing us to sneak in a bit of hurried conversation in our native tongue. "So, Juan, you're new, huh? Do you like our school, so far?"

"Yeah. A litt… Uh. Si…un poco," he finally answers sensing the approach of Mrs. V. He's sharp, quick thinking and not too shabby looking, either.   Neat crew cut, white, almost perfect teeth and long lashes to set off what I now see are gorgeous gray-green eyes.

The bell finally releases us into the raucous stream of kids in the busy hallway where we split off to different classrooms, waving adios to one another. I can't help noticing that he's just the right height and his jeans are rolled up precisely—as current cool dictates. Ohhkaaay.

So, John it is. I nod as I toss the lists into the basket that night. The situation isn't exactly perfect (he doesn't have a letter sweater or a class ring, it turns out), but it really doesn't matter because John has a—get this—a car!   It's more than I ever hoped for, especially since it runs— most of the time.

It's not that we don't have cars at our house—we do. They are everywhere, mostly in process.   A top shell and two car doors are on the back lawn, a frame with three wheels on the patio, two cars minus wheels on the driveway and one in the garage.   Jack has decided to be a mechanic and spends his weekends chasing parts and getting greasy.

Only one car runs all the time. But I'm not allowed to drive that car, ever since I backed into ol' Mizz Perkins' Cadillac down at Frudden's grocery store. It's was especially bad because it happened on the very day I passed my test and got my driver's license. I felt that sickening crunch and I jumped out of the car and ran five blocks, crying and choking and breathing hard until I collapsed on our front porch. I wailed and bawled and threw a block buster, gol'darn hissy fit. Daddy came out of the house, pulled the story out of me and then told me to get up from there, go back down to Frudden's, talk to Mizz Perkins and then get right back in our car and drive it home!

"No, Daddy, I can't," I blubbered. "I can't...you know...back up. You know it. I never could!"

"Oh yes you can, Miss Lily. You do it right now or I'll never let you drive again, you hear?"

Well, I did do it. But, he didn't. He told me I couldn't drive the car until I saved enough money to pay him back for Mizz Perkins' crumpled fender.

I can't believe my luck. A cute guy with a car. There's just one thing. The car is an ancient blue Chevy coupe, handed down from his grandfather, and it is drippy looking, no doubt about it. Jack tells me how it could be cool. "All it needs," Jack says, "is a paint job—gun metal gray primer and bricks in the trunk to lower it until it barely clears the ground. Man, be real sharp. 'Course if you had the bucks you could pay me to chop and channel it." Since I don't have the bucks, no sense wasting time on asking what chop and channel mean. Car language is almost as foreign as Spanish.

The plan is taking shape. John has to go on a trip with his family, and I convince him that I could sure use his car over the weekend. So, there it sits in our driveway, ready for the make-over. John will be so surprised and thrilled. I just know it. Jack buys the primer for me at the auto store with the money I've been saving to pay for the Mizz Perkins mistake. I find a bunch of old bricks behind the garage, and we're set.

Well, sort of. Jack tells me I have to do it because he has a job today down at the gas station. Heck, how hard can it be to spray a little paint and dump in a few bricks. It takes all day and two trips to get more paint. I have to admit though, it is a little tricky to figure out how many bricks to use to make it low enough, but I figure a couple of inches off the ground should do it.

Sunday afternoon and I'm so excited to show John. I drag him through the house and out into the back yard. "Ta-dah," I sing out and wave my hand along the car, like the used car salesman down at the Ford place. John is speechless. Oh, wow, this is great I'm thinking, button-popping proud of my hard work. "Cool, huh?" I gush.

John is gnawing at his thumb nail, those cute eyes wide in awe. Oh, this is just too good. I really surprised him! He rubs his eyes with the palms of his hands, then drops them on the knees of his jeans and hangs his head. Uh-oh.

Now, John is a quiet, easy going kind of a guy, so what happens next is quite a shock. Five swear words I never knew he knew spew out in a spitty stream. He stamps his foot, kicks at the grass and the gray green eyes are cold stone when he screams at me "Lily, you have no idea what you've done!"

He stomps over to the car, wrenches open the newly primered door, flops on the seat, turns on the ignition, floors the gas pedal and guns it out the driveway.

I guess two inches aren't enough. The back end screeches and scrapes along the pavement, ripping the bumper into a tangle as John tears off down the road.

I don't see how it could *all* be my fault. John never told me it was his grandfather's pride and joy. He never mentioned it was a true classic, a meticulously maintained authentic, in mint perfect condition— an eventual prize-worthy antique.

My steady no longer has a car. But he's still my steady. Mrs.Vardon sets it up on Monday morning when she lists off the pairs for conversation. "Lilita y Juan and remember no English."

I'm first to speak, pleading: "Perdona me, Juan. Por favor, por favor." I'm boring my eyes into his.

John melts. I can see it in his forgiving eyes. "Si, si Lilita." He says it softly in his ridiculously cute accent.

"Mucho gracias." I try not to blubber.

Quietly, oh so quietly and sweetly he answers: "De nada, mi Lilita."

Hard Times

This is a story I don't like to tell.

It's the last basketball game of the season, and if we win it, we'll win the championship—for the first time—ever. We're playing our arch rival, Livermore, and everyone in our whole town will drive those six miles over to their gym so our yelling section will be as loud as theirs. We hate Livermore with their bigger town and their bigger players and their big, big gym with trophies weighing down the shelves in their shiny showcase out in the hall.

We all put on our purple and gold letter sweaters and grab up our banners we made in woodshop, and we head out into the dusky, spring night. Mother and Daddy say they will meet me there because I'm going to ride with a bunch of kids.

Eight of us cram into Freddie's jalopy, two layers of us in the back. We scream and yell, waving our banners for the country side to see. We're singing out the school fight song and laughing up a storm. It's busy out here on the old two lane road to Livermore, everybody raring to go and raring fast. All of a sudden, Freddie—quick—jerks the steering wheel, and he swerves out into the other lane to pass a pokey tractor holding us up. He's stomping hard on the gas pedal.

The merry-go-round goes faster and faster, whirling and whirling until my head gets swimmy and little pictures like dreams fly by, all in technicolor with lots of sound, the volume turned up high. Then nothing.

Mother needs to tell the rest of the story, because I don't remember.

"Well, Daddy and I were just two cars behind you when the crash happened. Freddie's car and that other one coming the other way slammed, wham, right into each other, and they both were spinning all over and the rest of our cars piled up behind. I was screaming, and your Daddy kept trying to hold me back. But I ran and crawled over and under car parts and knocked away people in front of me to find you. I like to died, my heart beating so fast and my legs just barely holding me up. Oh Lordy, kids were everywhere, some hanging out of the cars, some in and some flung out over the road. I found you under a tree along side the road, knocked out, cut and scraped and bleeding, your shoes gone and your sweater hanging on by one sleeve and thank the Lord, you were breathing. Ambulances and fire trucks came blaring in with lights so bright I had to close my eyes. They carried you all to the hospital, and I told that Doctor I would stay with you no matter what he told me to do...even if I had to kick him in the shins. Oh, Lily, you were so lucky. They bandaged you up and gave you pills and when it was almost morning, they sent you home with us."

A lot of the other kids broke legs and arms and other stuff and can't come to school for awhile, like me. Freddie doesn't get to come back to school at all. He's still there, in a hospital bed... in a coma. Nobody knows how long he will lie there or whether he will die there.

Freddie's mom tells us kids to go visit him and talk to him because the doctor thinks he might hear us, and it could help him fight to wake up. It's a scary thing to do. But Elena and I go one day to the hospital. We need to hold hands to be brave enough. Freddie is tucked tight under a stiff white sheet and tubes are stuck to him with shiny white tape. Makes me shiver remembering that awful time in the white room where I had my tonsils taken out a long time ago. Freddie has the cutest twinkly brown eyes in the whole school and now they are shut down, the long lashes resting still on his cheeks. And his big dumb old grin has disappeared into flat line blue lips.

Elena squeezes my hand and nudges me a

little closer to Freddie's bed. I know she needs me to speak first because I am the talky one, and she is too afraid. My knees are wobbly and chest feels so tight I can barely breathe. I rest a little bit against the mattress and lean in close. "Freddie, hey Freddie. It's me, Lily, you know the big pest who's always nagging you to be on a committee or act in a school play or help on the yearbook. Well, now I'm going to nag on you to wake up. Come on Freddie, come on. We need you, no kidding, to be with us when we walk down the aisle in our caps and gowns. We just have to have you, you hear?"

"Yeh," Elena says in a breathy squeak, "please Freddie, please come back."

We stand there, our arms tight around each other's waist, warm glittery tears running down our cheeks. Eddie's machines make the only sound in the room for a long time until we get the strength to tiptoe out.

I'm trembling and my whole body is so cold I have to get into bed when I finally get home. I feel guilty, sick to my stomach, guilty. I can't quite figure why, but I do and it hurts so bad in my heart. I cry for Freddie and for Freddie's mother who talks every day to a son who never wakes up. I cry until my chest hurts and my eyes throb.

It's a crazy thing, but I suddenly remember when I killed the polliwogs from the creek, way back when I was little. After they died, I climbed into the sycamore tree and prayed for their tiny souls, me crying and hurting so bad—sick in a way I had never experienced before. That day, my mother gave me a word for this kind of pain. "It's called guilt, Lily," she had said.

Tonight when there are no more tears left in me, I ask her. "Mother, why did this have to happen?"

She lifts up my chin with her finger and looks straight into my raw and begging eyes. Her blue ones, the bluest on earth, are locked into mine. "It's called 'life' Lily and we can't ever count on it being easy."

Mrs. V

The Monday morning bell always seems louder somehow. The guys are hunched in a jeans-and-flannel-shirt clutch around Leroy Williams' desk. "Whataya take— purple or blue?" His pencil is poised over tally marks on a fat-ruled piece of note paper. "Okay, pony up. Fifty cents each." Leroy, the master of sly, silently slides the quarters and fifty-cent pieces into an old envelope just as Mrs.Vardon fills the frame of the schoolroom door.

Shushed, all nineteen of us turn to face the blackboard as if synchronized. Mrs. V's ample but stately form glides atop her black pumps down the aisle to her desk. All eyes are fixed on the coil of hair at the nape of her neck and the freshly-done sweep from her forehead.

"Blue," Leroy mouths behind her back, hoisting a thumbs up to three of the lucky guys.

You see, every last Saturday of each month, Mrs. Vardon lurches and bucks her big old Packard into the front parking spot of Edna's beauty parlor downtown. Her snow-white head of hair floats into the shop and the blue or...purple head sails out. We are never sure why it isn't always blue or always purple, but the suspense of it makes getting up the following Monday morning worth it.

Mrs. V teaches English, Spanish and Journalism—and French if anyone would ever sign up for it. She's tough, that lady. Teaches with a ruler in one hand and a baton in the other. She presides over us, standing at a pine podium, ordered up from Mr. Carter, our wood shop teacher. The baton taps out critical teaching points on the edge of it and the ruler marches around with her, maintaining student focus. Nobody messes with Mrs. V.

It's English today, and everybody is groaning and wailing about conjugating verbs and diagramming sentences. "God, Lily, how stupid is this? Who cares?" Elena whispers behind her hand.

"Hush, up Elena. The ruler is coming." Never would I ever tell anyone this, but I kind of like diagramming sentences and looking up vocabulary words and writing essays and even the verb stuff. I'm feeling pretty good about myself here, and I'm proud of the A- Mrs. Stingy Grader gave me last semester. So when the ruler walks over to my desk and peers at my essay, I'm smacking my lips at the thought of a compliment.

"Lily, look at me and straighten up while you're at it. Writing, *your* writing in particular needs work. Need to tighten it up. Your paragraphs need more structure, the over-all theme is too loose, and you don't make your points concisely. Well, actually, none of it is quite good enough." That one eye (the one that wanders off in a weird direction) is magnified behind her giant glasses and actually settles on me for a second. I have to stifle the flinch I feel coming on. When she nails you with that eye, you wither.

Hauling her body off in the direction of Leroy, she issues the order over her shoulder: "See me after school today. I'll design some special homework for you. "

Some homework! Ol' Vardon, the Warden means some *more* homework. Specially designed! Who does she think I am, some dummy? Heck, I know my stuff is better than anyone else's. Well maybe except Jeanette, the genius.

` Not only do I have extra homework, I have to do it in her room after school. Pages of dittoed exercises, a zillion re-writes, hours of reading essay examples on and on and on, everyday of the week. On Thursday, I wail to her back while she erases the blackboard, "Mrs. Vardon, why am I doing this? Why all this extra work? What did I do to deserve this? Why me?"

"Because my dear, no student of mine will

ever fail the College Subject A exam! You will pass with flying colors."

"Fail...how can I? I'm not even going to take the Subject....whatever it is."

"Yes, my dear. You will take the test. I will make it so."

Well, Mrs. Blue Head is nuts. She's gone over the hill, for sure. Me, take that test that smart kids take to go to college? Is that what she is saying?

"Mrs. V, I'm not..."

"Of course you are. I'll speak with your parents next week."

"But how? My family doesn't have money for college. Nobody ever goes to college in my family. I can't."

She wags her head, showing off the new blue glint. "You can and you will. I have ways. And, my dear Lily, so do you."

Tap, tap, tap snaps the baton against the shiny, piney podium.

Numbers and Space

It was in the Second grade when I first knew it: the big problem. It's art time. It should be fun. It isn't. Miss Fisher asks us to draw a picture of our school—the way it looks on the outside. I finish the large square building and manage to make the roof look like a triangle. Now I'm ready to make the stairs. There are lots of them. "They go up the side of the school," I whisper to myself. I can see them in my mind, but my pencil, clutched so tight my fingers hurt, won't—no—can't make the stair steps. My pencil just won't behave. The stairs finally appear on the page, looking like jagged witches' teeth— in and out— not up or down. "Go up, go up," I beg. How do I make the lines go up, then in, then up again? I erase and erase and try to copy Ralph Baker's perfectly and consistently upward treads.

I feel hot and red, the way I did when my sister and I were taking turns with a new tricycle she got for her third birthday. Little Nita could back up that trike out the driveway, around corners, into the garage, any place she wanted to go. I was six and a half and couldn't back up three feet without getting mixed up about how to turn the handle bars. I tried to tell myself, out loud, how to do it: "Remember, turn this way to make it go that way." It was so hard, and Daddy kept laughing at me and pointing like the school traffic patrol showing me where to go. I wanted to crash and smash the trike to bits. I tried and cried, out on that dusty driveway when I couldn't ever do it.

Backing up didn't work for me in arithmetic either. If I worked hard enough, I could add and multiply, but subtracting held the same mysteries and confusions as trike wheels did.

So, that's the history. This is now. Numbers and space and direction—still my crosses to bear. Geometry is my problem right now.

Mr. Patterson sits in his big wooden swivel chair, looking at me over his half-glasses. He's got my last test in his hand, sort of fanning himself with it. This is going to be bad…really horrible.

He clears his throat and leans into his desk. "Well, Lily. I know you studied. You always do. I know you try hard. You always do. But— you are failing."

Failure. Can't be me, sitting here, failing.We have some kids at school who are failures. They don't study, they don't try, they don't care. I get that. But there are kids who fail and can't help it. Like Edgar. Edgar is a big, lumbering, toed-in, foot-shuffling, sweet boy, whose coke-bottle glasses teeter near the tip of his broad nose. He carries his books around in a gunny sack and shows up everyday to sit in his seat for every class. I'm glad he thinks he is good-funny when kids laugh at him. I don't know what teachers do about grading him, but it doesn't matter because Edgar knows what he wants to do.

"Liii -lll- eey." He stretches out the syllables in my name, working around the flabby droop of his lips. "Know wha I wanna be?" I do know, because he tells me often. "No, what, Edgar?"

"A lah-won mow-er, jus like my Dad. He's gonna teach me, soons I grad-oo-ate."

And there's Bennie Souza. Bennie's family loves him, especially his mother who shows it with lots of food for Bennie to enjoy. Bennie wants friends. He really tries. But he just can't figure out how to do it. Bennie wants to read. He really tries. But he can't. Not won't.

I'm still thinking about my kind of "can't," when Mr. P gets up and walks over to his file. He brings back a green folder with my name on it and ruffles through some papers. "So, looks like you want to go on to college. That right?"

"Yeah, I guess so. I mean, I hope so. Mrs. Vardon says she will help me to find some scholarships, and I'm taking college prep classes."

My voice sounds pretty puny in my ears. We all know if you fail, you don't go to college.

Mr. P taps his lips with his pencil and looks up at me, slumped in my chair. "I don't get it. You've got good grades—nothing lower than a B. What's up with Geometry?"

"I never learned how to back up a trike, subtracting is a struggle, and I can't draw stairs either. Mr. P, I'm the one who doesn't get it. I just can't get it."

Mr. Patterson squints his gray eyes and rubs his finger alongside his nose. I hear two school buses pull out of the yard before he slams down the file, his eyes glittering a little. "Can't. That's not allowed in this class. Get out your book and stay awhile."

Every day, many, many days until the final exam, I stay awhile in Mr. Patterson's classroom. I'm not sure I'm really getting it, will ever get it, but I am doing it…maybe enough not to fail.

We're making a lot of clanky, shouting, guffawing noise while we clean out our lockers for the summer. Edgar comes up behind me with his book sack bumping along behind him. He's going to grad-oo-ate tomorrow. "Hey, Lil – ly." He beams his goofy, tilted smile, pokes me on the shoulder and asks: "Lil, know wha I'm gonna be?"

"Yep, Edgar, I do know. That's a good thing to be. Hey, know what *I'm* going to be when I graduate?" He cocks his heavy head. "Wha, Lil?"

"A college student, that's what Edgar." I wave the grade card in front of him. Smack in the middle of the line-up of A's for English, Spanish, History, Drama and Journalism is the big, beautiful , fat C- in Geometry. I'll never be sure whether it is gift from Mr. P or not. But on this day, his wide, wide grin and his crushing bear hug lead me to think that his joy is as great as mine.

Senior Year

The eight o'clock bell rings—seeming, perhaps, a bit inviting today. The double doors open— maybe a little wider, more welcoming than before. Locker doors clash and bang, announcing the fall semester of a new school year. It is the last for thirty-two of us. For us, Senior year is here. Seniors rule. Seniors rule the school. We've watched all those Seniors do it ahead of us, and now we'll do it, all of us ready to reign this first September day when we strut huge through the hallowed halls.

Mother and Daddy are mighty proud that I'm a Senior. "You made it Lil. You made it," they say. Then they wag their heads and rub their hands together smiling big at the thought of me graduating from high school. They never had the chance they say. Daddy made it through his Junior year in the every-grade-in-one-room school house back in Texas before he had to quit to help Granpa on the farm. Mother didn't even get to be a Junior. Her mother and daddy both got sick, and she needed stay home to take care of them and her six sisters and brothers.

What they don't talk about is me going to college. Maybe they can't imagine it. Maybe they have no way to think about it or to believe it will actually come to be.

But Mrs. Vardon knows exactly how it will come to be and is charging forward, pushing and prodding me every inch of the way. Mrs. V plays a big part in all of this senioritis ritual because she is our class advisor, our English IV teacher and faculty advisor to the yearbook, to say nothing of Senior play drama coach. She's silver-haired now—all the time. Sure takes all the fun out of Monday morning. Maybe she's too busy to make it to Edna's beauty parlor any more.

Mrs. V says I need to go visit at least two colleges I might want to attend. How will I do that? Mother and Daddy work every day of the week and taking off a day means a pay check that doesn't quite make ends meet. Mrs. V waves her hand in a quick "no matter" way and says she will take me.

Today we are going to visit UC Berkeley, Mrs. V's favorite because she says she got her Master's degree there—whatever that is. She picks me up in her old Packard heap. "Berkeley's not too far," she mutters as she lurches away from the curb in front of our house. Mrs.V has a heavy foot (to match her heavy body), and she presses it on the gas pedal in gasps and fits and starts. In, out, in, out—jerking us out onto the freeway. Whooee, it's a wild and scary ride. She lunges ahead, hardly ever looking to one side or other because her eyes are glued to the white line which seems to escape her every few minutes. Maybe it's that one off-kilter eye of hers, wandering around the way it does. I'm clutching the door handle until my fingers freeze up. Even I'm a better driver than this.

We do, however, arrive alive. Big, this Berkeley place. People jammed on the sidewalks, cars honking at the corners, stores nudged tight together up and down the streets. The campus is all over the place with tall, grey concrete buildings with blurry glassed windows marching around all those floors. We look into some classrooms. They remind me of the big halls where we all met that time for our Junior Statesmen state convention way down in Long Beach. Seems like a hundred seats in here, and they are all full. I almost have to squint to see the teacher who looks to be five miles away up there on the stage with a microphone. Cripes.

When Mrs. V bumps to a stop, back home in P-Town, one of the front wheels of the car jumps up on the curb by the Sycamore in front of our house. I hand her the UC Berkeley catalog. "I'm sorry, Mrs. V, I just can't do Berkeley."

She twists on the steering wheel and smashes the gas peddle on and off until the wheel thumps back down onto the street. The good eye looks in my direction.

"Well, Lily, perhaps we should talk about what you would like to study in school—your major, that is."

"Uh," I fiddle with the door handle a little. "I guess I don't really know, Mrs. V."

"I see. Perhaps...well, just tell me what you like to do. What you think you are good at."

"Talking, I really like to talk. It drives my folks crazy. Writing's fun too—and acting, doing plays, speeches, announcing—and oh yeah, I love to be in charge. Mother says I get the prize for being bossy."

Mrs. V's chin nods a little, and she waves her hand toward my door. "I will research the possibilities for our next trip, my dear. Ta, ta."

I get lucky on the next visit to college. Mrs. V isn't going to drive. It's a field trip for all of the CSF kids. The kids who aren't in CSF call it the brainy kids club. But I should tell them that it isn't brains that get you in, it's hard work. At least for me. So, we pile in the yellow school bus and head for Stockton where we are going to visit the College of the Pacific.

Instantly, I love this place. The buildings are brick, but softened by the ivy climbing all over walls and windows. Warm carved wooden doors invite you to come into the classrooms. There are trees and more trees with drippy leafy branches hanging down almost touching the green, green lawns. They are flooded with water that reflects the sky. Some students wave "hi" when they pass us by, and bells chime from atop a tall tower, spires pointing the way to puffy clouds. The air is warm and smells of the grass I see stuck to a mower parked under an oak tree.

We walk around the meandering campus, the student guide showing us the tall, gracious brick dorms, the library (more dripping ivy), and the chapel, illuminated inside by the sun glowing through the many colored glass windows. We have cokes in the Student Union and watch the basketball team practice their shots in the gym. And finally, wait until you hear this. It's purely a miracle. There is a college radio/TV station. My heart does the thumping thing. And I know right away when we peek inside that this is it! An actual place where I can do all the things I love—talk, act and write scripts and make announcements and...and...it is just too perfect! It fits me, and I will fit here. Finally fit. This will be my major and this will be my college.

Mrs. V is happy for me, her good eye twinkling. She will, she says, right away, start looking for scholarships, my dear Lily. Leave it to Mrs. V.

Year Book

The day when the year book comes out, and we actually hold it in our hands, we can taste the sweet finish, the end of high school for us. As soon as I get home that afternoon I wave the year book at Mother. "Where's the ruler, Mother?"

"What are you talking about? What do you need a ruler for? I swear, Lily, you make me worried sometimes that the bump you got in the accident left you a little...well, funny. Of course, now I think about it, you always were anyway, I guess. So go on. It's in the kitchen drawer next to the sink— if you just have to have it this minute."

"Ha-hah!" I giggle when I finish measuring in the year book. "Hey, Mother, come look at this." When she comes in, drying her hands on her apron, I show her the pages where each Senior has a paragraph naming all the things they did in high school, like clubs and sports and offices and awards and stuff like that. "Look here." I pull her over and tap the paragraph where genius Jeanette has her section. I line up the ruler along the left of the paragraph. "Two inches, right? Now, see this." I measure the lines on my paragraph. "Two and a half inches! Ta-dah!" I clap my hands, twirl around and execute a little bow.

Mother smoothes down her apron, using the flat of her palms, ironing with excruciating care. She picks up her dish towel. She motions with a flip of the towel to sit down on the couch. She stations herself across from me in Daddy's easy chair, but clearly not to lounge. Her back is a board, and the look on her face spells: serious subject.

Mother's voice is low, deep in her throat. "Lily, I can't believe you just did that. I am ashamed of you, bragging like that, showing off that you are better than someone else. First of all, it is just flat out wrong, and second, you'll find out if you keep doing that people will turn their backs on you and walk away. Why if there were eleven commandments and I got to write the last one, it would be 'thou shalt not brag nor boast.' Now, being proud is one thing if you deserve it and you can be proud—but just to yourself. You hear?" She slaps the dish towel over her shoulder and heads back out to the kitchen. Just about to turn the corner, she pauses and looks back at me. "But Lily, I can say it. I'm proud, real proud of you. Well, minus the ruler foolishness."

The last week of school, we run around crazy-like getting kids and teachers to sign our year books. Some just scrawl a name by their picture and others ask to borrow the book so they can take their time.

Elena takes her time all right. First she writes on the white blank page in the front of the book: "Reserved for Me." I guess she figures I'll know who that is. She covers the whole page with memories of all our wild times together, our double dates, boy friend crushes, twin clothes, the party in my garage, and the one in the mud. Then she squeezes in at the bottom: "To Be Continued." She crams the rest of it in pieces around the print on the Sports Activities page. There we are, both of us trying to look tall in the group picture of the Block A club, along with a few other girls and a lot of big, truly tall guys. She scribbles "Yeah!" over my head in the photo of me in my ugly pink gym suit posed with a hockey stick. The last little note is inside a heart and says, "The wedding date is set!" I am going to be her Maid of Honor, and I already have the yellow Swiss dot dress with the yards and yards of skirt held out wide with a new crinoline slip. I wonder if we will stay best friends and write and talk on the telephone forever. A small sad sigh escapes out of me all on its own, hinting maybe not.

Even the popular girls say nice things in the book like "You're a swell gal" and tell me how they are going to secretary school or beauty school or to a job down at the five and dime store.

John, my still steady boy friend, writes silly

things, and then a surprise. "Hey pickle puss, I just found out I am going to the College of the Pacific, too! Wow, what do you think about that?" I read this with a grin. And then an unexplainable little nag of concern creeps in. Ah, sweet John, I'm not so sure what I think about that.

The teachers write notes in the book too. They dash off, "Congratulations" and "Good luck" and "I liked having you in my class" and "I'll miss your crazy laugh."

Mrs. V writes a special note next to her picture on the faculty page. It begins "My dear Lily," and then goes on: "Your presence in my classes has been a trial and a never ending source of joy and inspiration. We are going to miss you, yet we know well that a good life lies ahead for you in distant fields. Shall we remember this: Give to the world the best you have and the best will come back to you.

Sincerely, your friend and teacher,
Helen Vardon."

Graduation

On graduation night, we line up outside on the wide rows of concrete stairs leading up to the auditorium. Girls are in white dressy dresses, standing prim, legs pressed together in shimmery silk stockings with feet faced forward in two inch heels. Elena and I duck down, checking to see if each other's black seams are straight. Boys, gawky in new suits and borrowed ties, sport black leather shoes shined to gleaming.

Picture taking requires frozen smiles, ordered up again and again by the futsy P-Town photographer. He is not pleased with the two fingered rabbit ears Leroy perches on the head of Too Tall Mary standing next to him. The ritual feels endless as the commencement jitters urge us to get on with it.

At last we are released into the hall where our caps and gowns await us. We hurry to be ready in two lines when our horn-honky, string-scrapey school orchestra sounds the first notes of Pomp and Circumstance. The Principal announces on the tinny microphone: "Let's have a big hand for the class of 1951!"

It's all such a misty blur, the ceremony and the speakers and the awards and handshakes over the scrolls of white diplomas tied in purple and gold ribbon. Of course, genius Jeannette is Valedictorian, and I pull in second, as usual, the Salutatorian. Her speech is perfect, precise—dry as a bone. Mine is terrific. But, mind you, I am only saying this to myself.

It's late, late when the parties are over, and we all head home, giddy from the excitement of the big day. Our house is still when I come up to the front door. Only Bootsie comes to greet me with his sticky, stinky old dog tongue. I flump onto the couch, the day's mementos sliding to the floor. I reach down to retrieve the year book, to find the page where Mrs. V had signed "your friend." My friend. I think about friends and best friends and boy friends. My memories linger over wise quotes and even Daddy's Ol' Eddards sayings and my mother's eleventh commandment.

Inching off the couch, I scoop up from the floor the treasures of my last ever high school event: the Spanish medal hanging from a thin braided rope, the tiny, hard-earned scholarship pin and the huge Bank of America silver plaque engraved in bold, black letters, "Speaking Achievement Award: Runner up." The slinky, golden tassel from the mortar board slithers through my fingers and the parchment diploma crackles when I uncurl it to peek one more time. Carefully and tenderly, from my sagging white dress, I unpin the browning gardenia presented to me by Mother and Daddy. I smile, remembering their glow of pride and happiness that cast brilliant light into the corners of our living room.

I tiptoe over to my cedar chest resting against the dining room wall. Opening it, the hinges creak as usual, but louder now in the sleeping house. I layer all of the treasures into the chest, but most reverently the year book, in the place of honor, nestled against the purple and gold letter sweater. I lower the heavy lid, finger tips carefully securing a hushed and gentle close.

Down the Road

The last dusty leg of this nostalgic trip will take awhile, but fortified with an iced latte in the cup holder beside me and a stack of CDs, it might not be too bad. I have forgotten how truly huge the state of Texas is. No wonder Texans have such gigantic egos.

So many memories swirl around in my head and line-up to be acknowledged. Out here on this barren country road, there is ample opportunity to think, to ponder, to reflect. And yes, to count blessings, too. Shall I share them with you? I'll tick them off.

In college I do find my place—where being different is not unusual. And I find my direction too, perfectly paired with what I like best to do—talk. Not on the radio or TV as it turns out, but (even better) helping those who have trouble talking, learning—fitting in. One successful college experience leads to another and another until all of the "school larnin" (Aunt Jewel would say) leads to a handsome certificate that awards the title "Doctor" before my name. Oh no, not the Doc Shanks kind. (I have no idea how to give shots or yank anything out.) It is the talking kind of doctor, the Professor kind. I do like to profess.

I have children who bring me joy and make me proud. (And by the way, they thoroughly enjoyed Christmas without the Santa Claus lie.)

I have grandchildren who are cuter and smarter than everyone else's. (I know, Mother, I just broke the eleventh commandment.)

I have a big hearted Italian husband who is only a tad short of being a full-fledged saint. (My father said that he would need to be, in order to live with me.)

Nita and Jack and I gather once a year at the lovely little green-grassed cemetery on a small knoll in Pleasanton, overlooking gentle hills, thoroughly covered with houses. The little hill where I sat and wept after losing the big speech competition, so long ago, now sports a mansion.

There are two bronze plates, side-by-side, identifying Mother and Daddy's burying spots. We putter around, pulling a few weeds and placing our bouquets above both plaques. We leave stones to mark our visit. I don't tell my sister and brother this is a Jewish tradition I learned about from a dear friend. We don't hold the same beliefs, my Texas relatives and me. I still don't fit there. But we tiptoe around the touchy subjects, so that we can enjoy our time together re-living old times and telling the same family tales over and over, lapsing a little, now and then, into back-home dialect, one that 75 years in California can't erase.

A rut in the winding road rouses me out of my reverie. It is blazing bright in this yellow and blue morning in middle Texas. As I round what I think is the last bend in the road, I tilt the windshield visor to get a better look ahead. There it is. The churchyard cemetery that I remember from a life time ago, presents itself in crumbling grace. I step down out of my cool car into Texas heat and spiky weeds poking up through the stones of the path. I meander, picking my way through the grave sites to the place where Granpa is resting in peace under a drippy-leafed mesquite tree.

I sit down, cross-legged, the grass itchy at the foot of the gray, granite marker. I unlock my lips. And I talk out loud. "Granpa, I'm here. It's Missy Smarty-pants, all growed up. Just letting you know, I can tell my own gol-dang stories now."

Acknowledgements

My gratitude to all those who supported and encouraged me in this writing adventure. They are:

. The Sonora Writers group who listened well, critiqued astutely and even, on occasion, applauded.

. Fellow writers who read drafts from early on to later stages: Blanche Abrams, Cheryl Brown, Phil Nichols, Tracy Barbutes, Judy Hewett.

. Writing teacher, Bill Manville, who taught me first...and best.

. Word Project Press: Patricia Harrelson, editor above and beyond, and Gillian Herbert, task master and helpful guide.

. My family, who gamely chipped in with bits and pieces.

. Most of all, my husband, "Saint" Ettore, who makes all things possible.

Nadine Pedron is Professor Emeritus, School of Education, Saint Mary's College of California. She taught and trained teachers in Special Education and Early Literacy. She developed and implemented literacy curriculum and staff development for school districts and conducted research in best practices for early intervention of reading problems.

She currently enjoys retirement with her husband in the beauty of the Sierra foothills.

6713546R00133

Made in the USA
San Bernardino, CA
17 December 2013